P. ALLEN SMITH'S
Garden Home

P. ALLEN SMITH'S
Garden Home

PHOTOGRAPHS BY JANE COLCLASURE

Clarkson Potter/Publishers
New York

Published by Clarkson Potter/Publishers, New York,
New York. Member of the Crown Publishing Group,
a division of Random House, Inc.
www.randomhouse.com

CLARKSON N. POTTER is a trademark and
POTTER and colophon are registered trademarks of
Random House, Inc.

Printed in Japan

Design by Jennifer Napier

Library of Congress Cataloging-in-Publication Data

Smith, P. Allen.
    P. Allen Smith's garden home.
    1. Landscape gardening. 2. Smith, P. Allen—
    Homes and haunts. I. Title: Garden Home.
    II. Title.

SB473.S575 2003   2002030717
712'.6—dc21

ISBN 0-609-60932-7

10 9 8 7 6 5 4 3 2 1

First Edition

To Gloria

CONTENTS

FOREWORD

FOR MANY YEARS NOW, WE HAVE OPENED OUR GARDENS

AT ARLEY TO THOSE WHO WISH TO VISIT THE ESTATE. ONCE IN 1985, MY HUSBAND, DESMOND, was on an early-evening walk when he met a young American student who was having a look round. It was nearly closing time, but they began conversing and my husband invited the young man back to our house to have a drink. This was the occasion of my first meeting Allen Smith and the beginning of a marvelous friendship that has lasted for many years and has brought me enormous pleasure. We started to talk and instantly found a tremendous bond because we shared so many ideas about gardens and garden design.

We have our differences. Allen is nearly fifty years younger than I am, and his garden in the hot, humid southern United States could not be more different from the cool, rainy atmosphere of Cheshire. Nevertheless, as our conversations developed, we found that we agreed on so many things. This communication across the generations and across the ocean impressed upon me most forcibly the fact that the principles of good garden design are both timeless and international.

In addition to our common interest in gardens, Allen and I share an enthusiasm for painting. Often when he visits, he brings me one of his own paintings and takes a look at what is on my easel. We then become absorbed in questions of composition, color, harmony, texture, and balance. But our talks about painting inevitably lead to more talk about gardens and planting. We both plan our gardens as though we were painting a picture. Looking at pictures and trying to understand what makes them successful is an essential guide to garden design and planting.

All gardeners have certain plants that have particular significance for them. My conversations with Allen frequently touch on these personal favorites, and we enjoy the opportunity to inspire each other. Many years ago, partly as a result of reading the delightful weekly articles of Vita Sackville-West, I became fascinated by the "old" roses, which I think have so much more character and charm than their modern progeny, the hybrid tea roses. I took great delight in introducing Allen to these wonderful plants, which I believe he now uses in his designs—climate permitting!

8

Gardening friendships frequently involve the exchange of plants. Allen, for his part, encourages me to grow American natives here at Arley, such as the charming three-cornered trilliums and the magnificent *Magnolia macro- phylla*. As I walk round my garden, the plants remind me of all the different people who have either given them to me or told me about them. I am delighted that some of my plants commemorate this remarkable transatlantic friendship.

Good garden design depends on surprisingly few principles; indeed, one might say that simplicity itself is of paramount importance. I was privileged to inherit a garden that had for many years benefited from a strong and sim- ple structure. The essential features are strong vistas that cross the garden at different angles, complemented by enclosures of varying sizes that create feelings of security and provide the element of surprise.

When I came to make additions and alterations to the garden, I was enormously assisted by the fact that it already had these strong "bones." Once you have established a strong structure, it becomes much easier to plan the planting schemes. Allen and I are of like mind over the importance of having a strong framework.

Making a garden is a way of expressing one's personality. Here at Arley we have many different small areas, each with its own character, created by a different member of my family. Five generations have made their contribution over the last 180 years.

As Allen and I exchange ideas, we are both constantly amazed at the similarity in our views and tastes. This beautiful book will give the reader an insight into the fundamental principles of garden design that helped to create not only the great gardens of England over the last three hundred years but also the lovely gardens in the United States that Allen himself has designed. Wherever you garden, whatever the climate, however large or small your garden is, I am quite sure you will find here the artistic inspiration and guidance to enable you to create a garden that fulfills your dreams.

Lady Elizabeth Ashbrook
ARLEY ESTATE, CHESHIRE, ENGLAND

PREFACE

OVER THE PAST TWENTY YEARS AS A GARDEN DESIGNER

I HAVE ENJOYED HELPING HOMEOWNERS CREATE PRIVATE SANCTUARIES FULL OF BEAUTY AND wonder. I find each garden to be a fresh opportunity to explore ways to create uniquely personal spaces. As I work with clients, they are often full of dreams and desires about the gardens they would like to create but are unsure about how and where to start.

In an effort to help them gain confidence in their abilities, I simply encourage them to think about making a series of outdoor garden rooms similar to those inside their houses. I find that when they associate designing a garden with designing and decorating rooms in their homes, they are comforted by the familiar and simultaneously excited about the possibilities. In thinking about their gardens as a series of beautiful yet functional outdoor rooms, they see how this approach could expand their living spaces with areas to play, rest, read, cook meals, dine, and enjoy a variety of activities.

These outdoor adaptations of interior spaces blur the distinction between inside and out, unifying both areas into one unit I call a garden home. This idea of blending the home and garden together as opposed to just making a garden grew in part from my response to the type of landscaping usually found in subdivisions. In these developments you commonly see house after house sitting in a sea of grass, encircled with the standard foundation plantings and an occasional flower or vegetable garden tucked in the corner of the yard. What a waste! Houses are expensive, and when you purchase one you are buying not only the dwelling but also the property that surrounds it. A garden home pushes the boundaries of a home's interior walls outside to include tastefully appointed garden rooms that are as comfortable and beautiful as a home's interior spaces.

As I developed this idea, I found there were many benefits for the homeowner. In very practical terms, this style of garden design adds a great deal to the curb appeal of a house. Any realtor can tell you that attractive landscaping increases a home's value. By creating a garden that begins at your lot line and blends with the look and style of your home, you will beautify your home's exterior and at the same time improve views from the inside.

This approach also creates more manageable-sized spaces around your home. Just as it would be difficult to organize your home's interior without walls and distinct functions, when you dedicate areas of your yard to activities such as dining or places to play, it becomes easier to envision the dimensions and style for each room.

Before clients grasped this idea, it was often a challenge for them to imagine how they could transform their yards into garden rooms. For many people, the area outside their homes was merely a lawn to mow or a place to walk across to and from their cars. When they began to think about creating a garden home, it was easier for them to see a whole new look for their property.

When setting out to design a garden, it is common for people to start by making lists of plants and tools. But before that, it is more important that you have a dream and the passion to create it. Otherwise, making a garden is a soulless endeavor that fails to satisfy.

As you add a series of garden rooms to the exterior of your home, you will look forward to spending more time in your garden, and your surroundings will lift your spirits. When you put yourself in places closer to nature, you are positively influenced by the setting. Why else would parks and picnic grounds be such popular destinations? When you create delightfully engaging places right outside your door, you are giving yourself a better chance to absorb the beauty and healing power of nature on a more frequent basis.

In today's fast-paced world, it is more important than ever to have places where we can connect with the seasonal rhythms of life. These soothing, eternal forces provide a sense of peace and stability not easily found elsewhere. Even in the smallest gardens we can establish a relationship with that touch of wildness that Thoreau called "the preservation of the world."

Gardens are powerful and magical places capable of transforming us. If you are willing to become involved in the process of designing, planting, and caring for a garden, then it can lead to new levels of self-discovery and transcendence. There seems to be something deep within us that needs to connect with nature by growing a garden. It is, after all, a long and essential tradition. When we recognize and honor this urge to plant and nurture, we are also cultivating a sense of well-being within ourselves.

If the Garden of Eden is the eternal metaphor for paradise on earth, then creating an aspect of Eden around our homes is a sure way to connect with the deep forces of nature and the even deeper energies within ourselves. In paradise, there is no distinction between inside and out. For these reasons, and many others that I'm sure you will discover along the way, I invite you to create your own garden home. In creating a place of wildness and beauty, I hope that you find a richness that restores and enlivens your spirit.

INTRODUCTION

CAN YOU RECALL YOUR FIRST MEMORY OF A GARDEN?

OFTEN THOSE EARLY IMPRESSIONS BECOME THE SEEDS FOR THE GARDENS OF OUR DREAMS. That was certainly true in my case. As I began designing gardens, I realized that some of my early experiences bubbled up in my drawings, shaping the way I envisioned the plans. As I recalled those memories, I discovered there were several key events that influenced my thinking. One of the earliest came when I was nine years old.

As a family, we had looked at farms off and on for a couple of years and finally we knew we had found the one. We all wanted it, even my mom. We were captivated the moment we laid eyes on it before the auction.

It was eighty-eight acres of rolling land complete with a farmhouse, barns, sheds, fence, pasture, crop fields, pond, and a clear running stream that flowed the entire length of the property. My younger brothers, Scott and Chris, had visions of catching stringers of fish from the creek, my seven-year-old sister longed for a horse, and I wanted a place for my own garden, just like my granddad's—a big garden, filled with everything: hills of squash, rows of corn, sweet potatoes, onions, and beans.

At auctions like this you could always count on refreshments and some kind of entertainment—music, raffles, contests—to hold the interest of potential bidders. As luck would have it, my brother Chris held the winning ticket for a door prize and was presented with a crisp new dollar bill. Later, as the bidding heated up for the sale of the farm and anticipation was at its peak, Chris waded through the crowd to find my father. Lifting up his lucky dollar and tugging at my father's pant leg, Chris yelled over the sound of the auctioneer, "Here, Daddy, will this help?" A big grin broke out over my father's face and with new resolve he went on to become the highest bidder. The farm was now ours.

Our new home was located in middle Tennessee on the Cumberland Plateau in Warren County. In 1969, when we moved there, it was a com-

OPPOSITE: *Drifts of springtime daffodils magically emerge from a pasture, long after they were planted.*

munity where everyone knew you by name. Farmers still brought their corn into the mill to be ground for feed, and Main Street was the place to shop every Saturday. My father loved farming and worked to instill his affection for the land into each of his children.

Dad had decided to move back to his hometown area after being gone for several years. When he returned with family in tow, changes were well underfoot that would transform farming in this region. Beginning in the late 1890s, there was a slow but steady shift from growing traditional crops of corn, tobacco, and wheat to growing ornamental trees and shrubs for the landscape and garden markets. By the late 1960s, the area was well on its way to becoming known as "The Nursery Capital of the World." A patchwork of fruit trees, shrubs, and shade trees grew right alongside grain, hay, and soybeans. Almost anyone who had even a small holding of land raised some nursery stock as a cash crop.

In the spring, acres of cherries, peach, dogwood, and redbud would bloom, creating solid blocks of color across the rolling hills. Of course, to the farmers and nurserymen, these ornamental plants were crops, not pretty trees. But seeing these large masses of color as a child made a strong impression on me.

I carved a patch for myself from my grandparents' garden and grew as many vegetables as I could. Family meals always included something from the plot. At supper we would name everything that we had grown—this ritual made our food all seem extra special.

Our new home was not unlike other rural communities around that time—slow-paced, directed by the rhythm of the seasons and each day's weather. It was a simple, uncomplicated life, rather ordinary in some ways, but stimulating to me.

I loved being outdoors so much that my mother always had a hard time getting me to

LEFT: *Home from college and on a visit to the farm, I have a laugh about my madras shorts with great-uncle Edward Smith.* OPPOSITE: *The Smith Farm at Dark Hollow, set in the gentle hills of the Cumberland plateau, is home to some of my earliest ideas about the landscape.*

come inside. Food and the setting sun were about the only things that would eventually draw me in. I was sure that all of life's real adventures were to be found beyond the walls of my home.

One of my favorite places to explore was Charles Creek. It was just a stone's throw from the front door of my house. One morning in late winter, I was walking along the creek on my way to a neighboring farm when I noticed a bright golden drift of flowers in the woods—it was a huge bed of daffodils, masses of them. They seemed to glow with their own light through the gray landscape.

As I approached to have a closer look, I noticed that the flowers were planted in rows lining what appeared to be a path leading to the remnants of an old house. A pair of half-crumbled stone chimneys stood at the ends of a dilapidated porch. Away from the house, I found the faint pattern of some large rectangles and circles outlining the boundaries of long-forgotten flower beds. More flowers followed along the line of an old fencerow. As I looked around I felt as though I had stumbled onto a golden treasure. The bright, fresh flowers waving happily in the breeze were a striking contrast to the decaying farmstead. I was sure it was an important discovery. I could not wait to race home and share the news.

A few weeks later, I went back to revisit my find. This time all that remained were clumps of green foliage, almost invisible on the forest floor; the daffodils had long since faded away. Upon seeing this transformation, I suddenly realized that I might have missed the flowers altogether if I had not been passing by just at the right moment.

In a blink of an eye, this garden magically bloomed in the woods, only to quietly disappear under the emerging canopy of leaves. By the looks of the decrepit farmstead, it had been quite a while since the bright flowers had been gathered to grace the family's table. The gardener had long since moved on.

The surprise and delight of finding that long-abandoned daffodil garden still glows in my mind, along with visions of the flowering hillsides and bountiful gardens of my family's farm. These experiences sparked a passion in me to create gardens that were so full of beauty and wonder, you longed to be outside. Along the way I also discovered I had a love and talent for drawing and painting. Expressing myself in this way lifted my spirits and brought me a sense of exhilaration similar to discovering that secret daffodil garden. I especially enjoyed drawing landscapes and flowers.

A trip to England in my early twenties crystallized all these events into a desire to become a garden designer. Shortly after college, I was awarded a Rotary Scholarship to attend the University of Manchester to study garden history and design. For me, this was like being sent to one of the world's greatest art museums to study painting.

While the entire English experience widened my heart and mind to what a garden could be, one event in particular had a strong impact on developing my ideas about garden design. As a part of my studies, I visited many of the country's grandest gardens that reflected centuries of tradition, creativity, and dedication. Late in the afternoon of an especially beautiful spring day, I was driving through the Cheshire countryside when I happened upon directional signs to the gardens at Arley Hall. I remembered the name from one of my classes, so I took the chance that there would be enough time for me to spend a few minutes in the garden before it closed.

Maybe it was the quality of light that evening, the time of year, or my solitary presence, but I immediately recognized that this place had a different and special feeling. The gardens lay mostly to one side of the large and grand buildings on the estate. As I began to walk around, I realized that I was viewing a series of well-defined garden rooms beautifully scaled in style and design to the manor house.

Because the light was fading, I would tell myself that I should go, and then I would see another path or gate that would draw me deeper into the garden. I found the suspense of what lay around the next corner to be thrilling. Suddenly, I came upon this incredibly stunning double herbaceous border 150 feet in length. I was bowled over by its splendor. The beds were full of perennials, many not yet

OPPOSITE: *Set in the pastoral landscape, Arley Hall has a gardening legacy dating back to the first quarter of the 18th century.* LEFT: *During one of my many visits to English gardens, my enthusiasm shows as I take in the scale of a yew hedge.*

in full bloom, but in their freshest green, with large alliums and towering delphiniums at the back, giving the entire space a cool, serene feeling. It was an enclosed area well proportioned by tall brick walls, clipped hedge buttresses, a long center lawn, glorious twin galleries of flowers, and at the end, a beautiful white garden pavilion beckoning me to come and sit for a while. It was absolutely breathtaking. I knew then I had to see it all.

One of the last places I visited was a grove that lay apart from the main garden. I was enthralled by its natural design. My trance was broken when I suddenly caught a glimpse of a solitary figure walking toward me. As he drew closer, I could see that it was a man with a cane, walking slowly, enjoying the moment just as I was. Soon he was near and I felt compelled to say, "Beautiful evening, isn't it?" He replied, "Yes, quite." This brief exchange led to more conversation about the garden. "You know, my wife is very interested in gardens and I would like for you to meet her," he said. I assumed he and his wife were also admiring visitors, until he said, "Oh, by the way, my name is Ashbrook, and this is my home."

This chance encounter led to an invitation to come by the house for drinks. There I was introduced to Viscount Ashbrook's wife, Lady Elizabeth Ashbrook. From the moment we met, our conversation was filled with talk of gardens, favorite plants, successes and failures, as well as philosophies of design. This was to be the first of many wonderful exchanges between us.

I came to understand why Arley was different from many of the other English gardens I had visited. This was a family garden. From its establishment in the early 1700s, members from each generation had enhanced its beauty by adding their own personal touches. Amid a framework of brick walls, clipped hedges, and iron fences each garden room reflected the unique design of the gardener who conceived it.

The walled gardens dated from 1743, when Sir Peter and Elizabeth Warburton came to live at Arley. In 1846,

Rowland and Mary Egerton Warburton created much of the garden's framework, a design that remains to this day. More recent additions include the intimate and secretive flag garden created by Antoinette Egerton-Warburton in 1900 and the walled garden designed by Lady Elizabeth Ashbrook in the 1940s.

I was deeply impressed by the stewardship expressed by the care each generation contributed in passing along this living legacy. The garden was not only for pleasure; it was also useful, with rooms housing an orchard, a greenhouse, and vegetable gardens. Together these areas created a beautiful transition between the estate and the surrounding agrarian landscape, a kind of "half home, half garden" area unifying the manor house and the surrounding property.

While few of us inherit three-hundred-year-old gardens that have been lovingly passed on through generations, we can create our own garden homes that inspire us by following the same basic principles that guided the masters.

That is exactly what I did when I returned home from England. I began creating gardens that intentionally blurred the line between indoors and out, places of wonder and beauty worthy of enjoyment today and for many tomorrows.

You can do the same with your garden. As you read in the next section about how I created my garden home, I hope it will inspire you with thoughts and dreams of how you can create your own.

OPPOSITE: *A friendship made in the garden. Lord and Lady Ashbrook and I enjoying an afternoon among the roses.* LEFT: *The alcove serves as a focal point and a destination to view the double herbaceous borders at Arley.*

MY GARD

EN HOME

"ARE YOU STILL LOOKING FOR A HOUSE?"
ASKED A FRIEND WHO CALLED ME QUITE UNEXPECTEDLY ONE
DAY. "WELL, I KNOW WHERE THERE IS ONE YOU CAN HAVE FOR NEXT TO NOTHING!"

She had my attention. Of course, I was interested. Who wouldn't be, especially since I had been looking for a house to restore? So without hesitation, we agreed to meet and have a look. My friend was right: The owners had other plans for the lot where the 1904 Colonial Revival cottage was located, and they intended to tear it down if a suitable steward could not be found. The house could be mine if I agreed to move and restore it.

I knew this was the house for me the moment I walked inside. I loved everything about it. Its tall ceilings, hardware, floor plan, and pocket doors were all original and intact, and the exterior of the house would make a perfect backdrop for a garden. There was no doubt that it would need a lot of work, but it was structurally sound and full of potential.

Soon, I found some property and a house mover. The new location was ideal. It was a double lot in a historic neighborhood, and the scale and vintage of the house would fit comfortably in the area. Since the land was on a street corner, moving the house into position would be easier. The extra room would also give me plenty of flexibility for siting the house and garden.

Wild vegetation had happily covered the lot since the original house was pulled down sometime in the 1970s. At one time, some well-meaning neighbors covered the area with six inches of gravel in an attempt to transform it

into a neighborhood park. All of this had to go. When the bulldozer was finished, there was nothing left, except for one large oak tree in the back. While others said it looked barren and pretty pitiful, I saw it as a clean slate, a natural tabula rasa, on which to paint my picture.

After creating countless gardens

LEFT: *A pair of red maple trees 'Red Sunset' frames the entry to my front garden. As they grow they provide relief from the western sun.*

for friends and clients, the day had finally arrived for me to design my own. I was exhilarated by the idea of putting into place many of the concepts I had developed over the years. I already knew that I wanted to surround the entire house with a garden and plant every square inch of the property, but I had to have a plan.

Time and again, I had witnessed how homeowners acted on their first impulse to jump ahead rather than taking on the process methodically. I, too, had to resist the desire to start planting trees and creating flower beds. I saw this house and garden as a model that could help me become a better designer and more effectively assist others with their own designs.

My ideal garden home would be a place where the house and garden were blended together into a unified whole. A series of outdoor garden rooms would begin at the walls of my home's exterior and extend all the way to the lot line. In this way I would expand my home's living space by using my entire property. My goal was to create the same level of privacy, intimacy, and function that I had inside my home within these garden rooms. This would give me comfortable areas where I could reconnect with nature and foster a greater sense of place.

ABOVE: *The day I moved the house onto the lot was my moment of greatest doubt. I wondered what I had gotten myself into, and so did my neighbors!* (Photo by John Woodruff)

23

One of the first things I had to consider was how to position the house on the property. So often when I am called in to help with the design of a garden, the house is already under construction. By getting started before the foundation is laid, I can often show them how just a slight repositioning of the structure can create better spaces for the garden.

So, when my house came rolling down the street on a cold January day in 1989, I had already spent considerable time working out exactly where it would sit on the lot. One of the most useful moments in conceptualizing my plan came before I even moved the house. To relocate the dwelling from one historic district to another, I had to gain approval from the city's planning and zoning board. I was required to submit drawings of how I intended to site the house on the lot and landscape around it. So before the house could be mine, I had worked through every possible scenario.

I made a cutout of the footprint of the house and moved it around on the survey plan. This helped me visualize the garden spaces around the dwelling. Eventually, I decided to shift the building into the southwest corner of the lot, which seemed to offer the most potential for garden rooms, to create a good balance between private and public spaces.

From there I began working out the various outdoor rooms I wanted around the house to see how they related to one another and to the house itself. The shape of the house and the lot created a series of rectangular spaces. One

ABOVE LEFT: *Hedges, looking raw and immature, and brick borders were the earliest bones in the garden.* RIGHT: *Today, the entry arbors and fence are in place and the hedges and roses are full grown.*

long rectangle ran across the front of the property, two others along each side of the house, and another along the back. With this arrangement, I recognized an opportunity to design strong, unbroken lines of sight or axes from one garden room into the next. Like an open door, these visual sight lines would allow visitors to stand in one room and see directly into the next.

After positioning these openings through portals or entries, I further divided

the rectangles into nine garden rooms and began to imagine how each space could have its own personality yet remain a part of a cohesive whole. As I laid out this plan on paper, I added an entire circuit or path that looped around the house, connecting one garden room to the next.

From here I imagined hedges and fences that would serve as "walls" for each room, with arbors and gates as "doorways." At this stage I like to lay out a garden's framework as large blocks of various shapes and sizes before I think about which plants to use or worry about other details such as color or materials. In this case, the method resulted in a plan that was detailed and instructive enough to gain approval for moving the house and general enough so I could have some flexibility in refining my choices in the future.

Whenever I design a garden, I find inspiration often comes in unexpected ways. My own garden was no different. To make sure the house could fit under electric wires and was narrow enough to roll down the street, the roof and all of the porches had to be removed. Once it arrived, I stood looking at this forlorn shell perched upon the bare lot—not exactly a pretty picture. But surprisingly, seeing the house and property in this "stripped down" state allowed me to stand back and visualize what I needed to add to unify the look and style of my house with the garden. I began seeing porches, arbors, gates, and roof angles that would all work together. I also walked through the house and looked out the windows to decide what surrounding views I wanted to enhance and which ones I wished to screen.

Now, more than ten years later, my garden still has its original framework of rooms. And just as I adapt the inside of my home to my changing needs, my outdoor rooms have also been a work in progress, providing me with a series of "studios" where I experiment with new colors, textures, and features.

To give you an idea of each room's character and function, I offer a tour through each area.

ABOVE LEFT: *The fountain begins to take shape with circular forms made from strips of plywood. Note the small holly plants that will later become the hedge.* RIGHT: *Today a collection of potted plants, white roses, and perennials fill the fountain garden. A holly hedge* (Ilex cornuta 'Needlepoint') *defines the perimeter and encloses the space. These living walls make this one of the most private rooms in my garden.*

The Front Garden

AS YOU ENTER THE GARDEN FROM THE SIDEWALK IN FRONT OF MY HOUSE, YOU WALK through a double picket gate and step into an area significantly shallower than it is wide. A brick walk leads up broad wooden steps to the front porch and entry. A picket fence and plantings define the remaining "walls" of this garden room. It is an enclosed space that is only fully revealed once you step inside.

The space has a slightly formal feel, reflecting the 1904 Colonial Revival architecture of my house. To the right and left, at each end of the long lawn, are focal points. To the left is a large cast-iron urn draped with three large evergreens. To the right is a simple bench that beckons visitors to enjoy the view. This room corresponds with the entry hall in my home, a viewing station to orient visitors to the rest of the garden.

If you have held a memory of a place in your mind and always wanted to re-create it, you will understand the inspiration behind my front garden. For me, it was the memory of those stunning double herbaceous borders I encountered at the Arley Estate during my student days in England. The inspiration for classic English flower borders first came from modest cottage gardens, so it seemed applying some of the same qualities would be right for my cottage-style home.

Originally herbaceous borders were designed as ways to display and organize the plants in more harmonious combinations. Ironically, many of the most favored plants used in these English borders are native to American meadows and prairies. On subsequent visits to England, I have found goldenrod, purple coneflowers, and towering joe-pye weed as well as phlox, spiderwort, rudbeckia, and asters—patches of color amid tapestries of greens and grays.

LEFT: *Like a long gallery in a museum, the lawn between the borders in the garden at Arley invites the visitor to view the flower "paintings" along its length.* OPPOSITE: *In May, rose blossoms dominate my garden. This front garden room is where I display many antique varieties from my heritage rose collection.*

However, for my cottage garden, the classic English double perennial border would not work, but by duplicating elements of its form, I could create a similar look. Instead of the tall brick walls and yew hedges used at Arley, I planted a holly hedge and built a picket fence to contain the volume of space. And rather than plantings of only herbaceous perennials that would die to the ground in winter, I chose flowering shrubs, trees, and perennials to create interest throughout the year. Since the area was small, I limited the color palette to purples, magenta, all shades of pink, and lavender, accented with white.

Once the picket fence went up, I lined out the flower borders and began to enrich the heavy clay soil with manure, sand, and compost. The first year I planted cosmos, vinca, cleome, cockscomb, and salvias. These, along with purple fountain grass and morning glories that scampered up twig trellises, made a triumphant splash—the wildness and waves of color that first season resembled the paintings of Claude Monet.

Over the next few seasons I continued to rely on annuals to fill in as the shrubs and perennials became established. I also started an old-fashioned rose collection in this area. In early spring, the first wave of bloom begins with bulbs—hyacinths, tulips, and alliums. Next, the earliest roses unfold, and the color and fragrance build with other flowering plants until the roses peak sometime in May. Then summer- and fall-blooming perennials take center stage, along with a few annuals, until the curtain comes down with the first frosts.

A dominant feature in this garden is an arbor entry that supports the white climbing rose 'American Beauty' and leads you into the fountain garden. The columns, similar to those along my front porch, blend the style of the home and garden.

The arbor is framed within a tall clipped hedge that creates a solid green wall, blocking the view of the room beyond. I am always delighted when visitors ask, "What's through here?" as they walk toward the arbor, because it is just that aura of mystery that I am aspiring to create.

The Fountain Garden

AS YOU PASS THROUGH THE ARBOR IN THE MORE FORMAL FRONT GARDEN INTO THE FOUN-tain garden, the mood changes. Here, a seven-foot-tall evergreen holly hedge defines the walls of the room, giving the area a quiet, private feel. The further you move inside, the more intimate in size and style the rooms become, just as you would find in most homes.

I designed the fountain garden to reflect the atmosphere of my library, but in this case, the plants serve as the volumes on the shelves. Because I am an avid collector of plants, one of my garden home's most important features is to accommodate my ever-growing collection. This is my favorite outdoor room for trying new perennials, bulbs, and annuals within its clearly defined framework. Like the indoor library, it is a comfortable place to sit and examine the plants and spend time relating their characteristics to one another.

When I took the design of my fountain garden from paper to reality, I knew the walls and paths within the room would have to project a certain precision—there is something about a solid framework in a garden that puts us at ease. It contains, it directs, it screens, and it helps us to organize our responses to the space both consciously and subconsciously. Perhaps the appeal of defined boundaries lies in our need for structure and order in our lives.

To help me establish the size of the enclosure, I looked for logical clues from the site. For instance, when I laid out the boundaries, I used the distance between my

RIGHT: *The view looking west through the rose-covered arbor into the fountain garden.* OPPOSITE: *In late summer, salvias and nicotiana step forward in the border, offering a last splash of color before the onset of fall.*

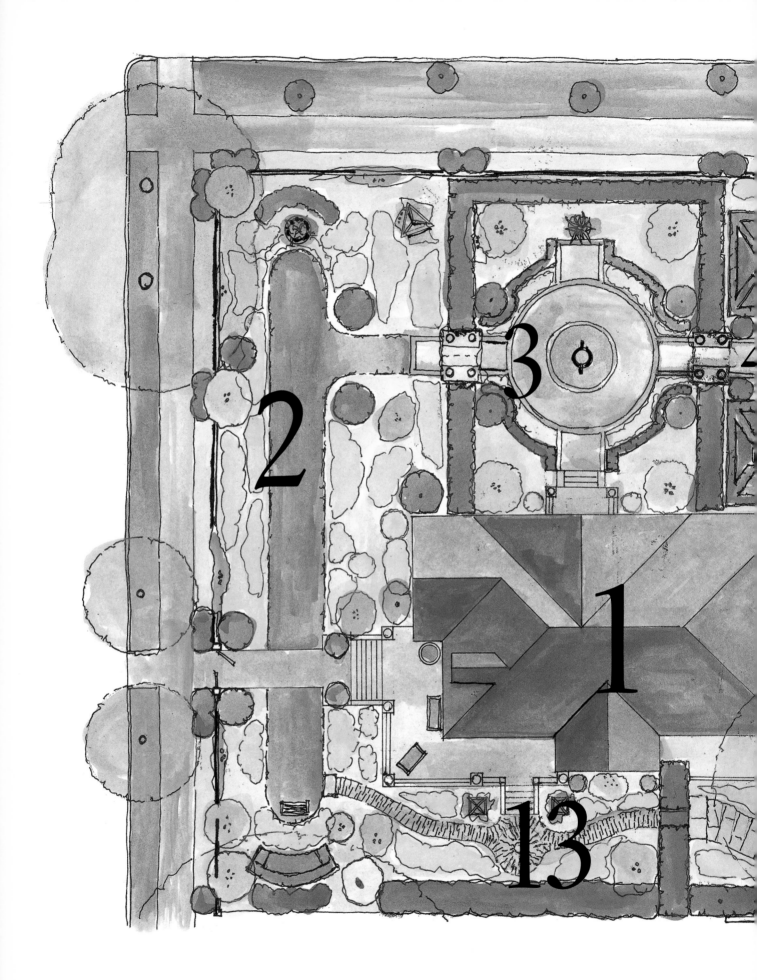

This bird's-eye view of my garden home illustrates the series of garden rooms surrounding the house. Like my interior spaces, each of these garden rooms has its own character, style, and function. A connecting circuit of paths and walkways directs the flow from one room to the next.

KEY TO PLAN
1. House
2. Front garden
3. Fountain garden
4. Parterre
5. Rondel
6. Vegetable garden
7. Toolshed/chicken house
8. Loggia
9. Garage
10. Service yard
11. Alley
12. Shade garden
13. Hallway garden

ABOVE: *These three garden rooms on the north side of my home greatly expand my living space all the way to the boundaries of my property.*

RIGHT: *These arbors provide punctuation in my garden, directing the visitor from one garden room to the next. Rose 'White American Beauty' (or 'Frau Karl Druski') fill the bonnets above, making them even more eye-catching.* OPPOSITE: *A bird's-eye view shows the progression of my garden rooms. The contrasting greens of boxwood and artemisia 'Powis Castle' accentuate the simple X design of the parterre garden.*

house and the sidewalk to determine its width. To establish its length, I found its center point by aligning it with a major gable on the roof of the house. From this point I measured to the nearest corner of the house and then used that same distance in the opposite direction to establish its full length. That measurement was nearly the same as its width, so it created a simple geometric shape, almost a perfect square, to fashion a garden within.

To arrange the hedges in a straight row I stretched a string and dug a trench along the line rather than plant the shrubs in individual holes. With this approach I could backfill the trench with a good rich blend of topsoil, compost, and manure. A total of thirty plants spaced thirty inches apart made the room—a space bounded on three sides by the hedge with the house finishing the square.

Using shrubs as the living walls and borders of a garden room is often less costly than masonry walls and fences. The downside is the time it takes to reach maturity. The *Ilex crenata* holly hedge around the fountain garden took five years to grow tall enough to reach the seven-foot height I wanted. While this required plenty of patience, cow manure, and shearing, the hedge now offers the sense of unity, boldness, and containment I had envisioned.

Soon after the hedge was planted, I began laying out the pattern for the walk. I wanted, within this square room, to create a circle that would eventually become a water feature. The hedge was a given, but how about the interior? How should it present itself? First, at the suggestion of a friend, I considered a single large tree in the center, but what about my dream of water? Ultimately, I decided to create the design in stages. For the first five years I made a planting bed in the center circle with four flowering trees to punctuate the corners and four conical hollies to accent the entries. Later, I replaced the bed with a circular water feature.

In its initial stages, this garden, like the rest of the property, looked raw, and I'm sure, to the passerby, without promise. I pressed on and poured the footings for what would be the borders and outline of the paths until my budget would allow me to buy the bricks and construct the water feature. I knew that if I didn't lose sight of my dream and took the improvements a step at a time, I would eventually achieve my goal.

The clearly defined lines of the walk and hedge established order and provided a necessary foil for the exuberance of plantings that one day would follow. Setting up this tension between two opposites gave life to the design.

As you enter the fountain garden through the pillared arbor, you step onto a gravel path that divides to encircle the water feature and then merges on the other side where a matching arbor invites you to exit. This arbor frames the view of a toolshed in another garden room, creating a focal point that entices you to explore more of the garden.

The Parterre Garden

UPON LEAVING THE CIRCULAR GRAVEL PATH IN THE FOUNTAIN GARDEN, YOU STEP ONTO A brick walkway that leads through the parterre garden. From the French *par terre*, "on the ground," a parterre is a simple pattern on the surface of the garden made with plants, usually evergreens. These designs emphasize the ground plane of the garden. Parterres can be as elaborate as those in the most formal seventeenth-century garden (called *parterre de broderie*), or they can be simple geometric patterns of clipped low-growing shrubs or designs made with raised beds in a vegetable garden.

To develop my parterre, I planted boxwoods in matching patterns on either side of the walkway. This area acts as a brief visual transition between two larger garden rooms. The path is about ten feet long with rectangular twenty-foot beds extending out on either side. The parterre creates twin grids that offer a framework to plant within.

The combination of formal and informal shapes in this area makes a good marriage. Shaped boxwood hedges, highly formal in themselves, act as a visual foil to the effusive tumble of perennials and flowering

annuals planted around and amid the shrubs. This is particularly true in high summer when everything seems to grow overnight and the biggest challenge is bringing visual order to a riot of growth and color. Without a few formal elements, my garden would lose its sense of balance.

In spring, tulips emerge through underplantings of gray foliage artemisia. I alternate the plants in this area. In some years I have filled it with larkspur, bachelor's buttons, and poppies, and at other times I have let it lie fallow.

The grid pattern radiates toward the center, drawing the eye to a strong upright trellis covered by the white rose 'New Dawn' and clematis. These plants are beautifully cast against the dark holly hedge "wall" of the neighboring fountain garden. I like the dynamic look of vertical elements rising suddenly out of a low, flat plane.

Like the holly hedge in the fountain garden, the boxwoods require shearing twice a year to maintain their shape—once in the early spring before the new growth appears, and again in midsummer. Not only are these evergreen elements essential to the framework of the garden, but as the plants mature, they can become a place to have some fun by pruning them into more compelling shapes.

The path has a single step up to the next garden room. When the site allows a change in levels, a step in the path interrupts the walking rhythm and provides a sense of entrance as visitors move from one area to the next.

The Rondel Garden

THE RONDEL GARDEN IS MADE UP OF A LARGE OVAL LAWN ANCHORED BY FOUR MATCHING crab apple trees. A rondel is a type of fifteenth-century French short poem. In the eighteenth century, the English adopted the term to describe a circle or circular object such as a tower or the shape of a garden area. My rondel is actually more elliptical than circular, positioned so that two sight lines intersect at its center. The first is aligned with a view from the fountain garden through the arbor to the toolshed. The other can be seen when walking through a side entry. This arbor frames a view across the length of the lawn toward a covered breezeway or loggia.

The rondel naturally seems to invite relaxed conversation, meals, and gatherings; it reflects the den in my home. The tables and chairs in this room are moved regularly, and it has the most foot traffic and use. It's the place I'm most likely to sit down and put my feet up. From the beginning, an elliptical form just seemed to rest gently in the space, lending a sense of order and reassurance. Beyond the shape, I wanted a lawn large enough to accommodate a small ten-by-ten-foot tent for entertaining.

This garden room recalls my childhood and the old orchards I once played in. Long before the lawn was in, I anchored the corners of my orchard with four 'Narragansett' crab apples. Then came a row of boxwood that outlined the shape of the space. My goal was to repeat the oval shape as often and as subtly as I could. It worked, but never so well as when I added a stone border separating the lawn from the planting beds. This brown line of stone helps create an even sharper distinction.

Each year, as the crab apples have matured, they have become the most outstanding feature in this garden room. Their limbs bring a sensuous movement to the space. In certain places the limbs of the canopy have "knitted" together, forming a ceiling to the room and creating an interplay of light and shadows on the ground.

Over the years, the selective removal of smaller limbs, isolating certain ones and removing the others, has added strength and structure. From the center point of the

RIGHT: *The center of my rondel garden marks a major cross axis. In spring, a flurry of white crab apples and an abundance of tulips transform it into an enchanted place.* OPPOSITE: *I started the parterre design with tiny boxwood plants a few years ago and shear them only twice during the growing season to keep their shape and form.*

oval, the views in each direction are framed by the canopies of these trees. In spring, the bed beneath their branches hosts a generous display of tulips. Bold drifts of almost any plant are far more effective than one or two of anything, but this is particularly true of bulbs. And by keeping the plantings simple—one theme and one color—I can make the best visual impact. Natural drifts are always very pleasing to the eye; they look like colonies of plants, similar to what you would find in the wild, appealing to our subconscious understanding of the natural world. The tulip display is always such a brief moment, but worth the effort when they all come into bloom with the crab apples showering them with petals from above.

The Vegetable Garden

LOOKING TOWARD THE BACK OF MY PROPERTY, BEYOND THE RONDEL AND OVER THE BOX-wood hedge, you glimpse the vegetable garden. This is one of my favorite areas not only because it was one of my first gardens as a child but also because it responds to both my practical side and my love of beauty. Here I grow armloads of fresh produce in a small space that is rich with pattern and texture.

This area corresponds in feel to the kitchen in my home, and just like my indoor kitchen, this room is furnished with a table and a place to wash the vegetables. Like the compartments of my refrigerator, a series of raised beds in

ABOVE LEFT: I love getting out and work-ing in my vegetable garden. It's where I receive the most reward for my efforts.
RIGHT: An aerial view of my toolshed and raised vegetable beds, which produce enough for me and then some to share with friends.

my kitchen garden establishes order and keeps the various groups of vegetables separated. In early spring the beds are filled with broccoli, sweet English peas, onions, and lettuce, and by summer the same beds give way to tomatoes, peppers, and basil.

To parallel the cabinets and drawers in my kitchen that hold the eating utensils,

I built a garden shed between the two growing areas. Inside I store the trowels, forks, and other tools of the garden. The shed has a dual purpose: Part of it also serves as a home to my small flock of chickens that provide me with a steady supply of fresh eggs.

My kitchen garden area was clearly too small for crops that demand space, such as corn, squash, and potatoes. It was better suited for smaller edibles such as tomatoes, broccoli, peppers, and a range of salad greens and herbs. In the beginning, before I built my arrangement of four-foot-square raised beds, I planted seeds and plants in small blocks. Over the seasons, I tried several different patterns before arriving at just the right design.

Containing these blocks in raised beds brought style and order to the area. The effect went beyond the look—it made me get even more excited about my vegetables, herbs, and flowers because the space seemed more manageable.

I could plant an entire raised bed in a short amount of time and then move on to the next, or return to it later. Like the boxwood parterres, the pattern of the borders of these raised beds created visual interest in all four seasons, whether planted or not.

This tiny garden evokes a certain nostalgia in me. I suppose it takes me back to the farm of my childhood. The orchardlike feel of the crab apples, the vegetables, the honeybees, and the bantam chickens all help to keep me connected to my agrarian past. Its location near the back door and the kitchen makes it easy to access and helps me to view the garden and kitchen as connected and better integrated.

There is a psychology of use in a garden. It is pointless to arrange the paths where you have to go out of your way or around some barrier to use the space. Moving through a room must be convenient and comfortable. I have learned to place paths and site things where I will use them, not for the sake of decoration or effect.

ABOVE LEFT: *The even temperament of bantam chickens called Cochins (originally from China) makes them well suited to a small garden, and their waste is added to the compost.* RIGHT: *All of my vegetables are organically grown in soil enriched with homemade compost each time I plant.*

The Loggia

FOLLOWING THIS PHILOSOPHY, THE PATH from the kitchen to the kitchen garden is through the loggia. Connecting the house to the garage, this covered breezeway satisfies my desire to have an outdoor dining pavilion. Since the day I finished laying it out, the space has been equipped with an old drop-leaf dining table and eight chairs. Whenever the weather allows, it is my favorite place to have meals, whether alone or in the company of friends. The room is accessorized with wall sconces and wire baskets for lighting, ceiling fans to stir the breeze, and sisal rugs to give the space an even greater feeling of a room.

In spring and summer, I fill it with houseplants, pillows, candles, and magazines—all the creature comforts found in the most pampering of rooms. It is also a multipurpose area frequently used as a work space. Here I arrange flowers, write, repair my beehives, and paint.

From this room there are views of the rondel (to the north) and the shade garden (to the south). This breezeway helps to make the transition from one distinctly different garden room to the next, and it offers a place to enjoy the garden completely protected from the elements. I find myself wanting to spend entire days in this space, occupying myself with projects or simply resting as I take in the garden around me.

From the loggia, a stone path follows around and under the massive oak tree that is the central feature of the shade garden.

The Shade Garden

THE TINY SHADE GARDEN IS FILLED WITH WOODLAND NATIVES THAT HAVE BEEN ARRANGED with a free and inexact hand. A screen of evergreens and hornbeam blocks the view of the neighboring house and the service yard on the south side of the garage. A path curves through the area in such a way that you cannot see the entire garden without walking further down the path. This helps to create a sense of mystery as to what lies beyond. Once you walk along the path, a long corridor running along the side of the house will come into view, broken by a tall, formally clipped hedge with an arched passage through it.

Contained by hedges and the house, this garden is filled with an array of loose natural shrubs such as philadel-

phus, rhododendron, azaleas, and hydrangeas. Although I call it my shade garden, it is in fact a place of varied light. Here I can grow a dazzling display of tulips each spring using a large cast-iron container as a focal point to catch the eye.

The walk through the shade garden was turf in the beginning but was eventually upgraded with large flagstones. The wonderful thing about paths is that they can always be improved. All of the paths in my garden have gone through transformations as part of my garden's ongoing evolution. The slight curve in the path stirs a sense of mystery, and the clipped hedge and arch discreetly conceal the view beyond.

On this side of the house I relaxed the lines and the mood, taking my lead from the large shady oak tree. Here, soft undulating forms felt more like a woodland. This natural, less rigid feeling contrasts with the axial paths and the arrangement of space in the front, fountain, and rondel gardens. The bed around the oak is full of bulbs—species

tulips, scillas, and miniature daffodils dominate in the spring and then make way for nerines, autumn crocus, and colchicums in the fall.

The Service Yard

JUST AS YOU BEGIN TO WANDER DOWN THE STONE path at the curve in the shade garden, a secondary path of stepping-stones leads into the service yard, which is the equivalent of that place of utility for the mechanics of daily living (a mudroom in my case) found in every home. Tucked away behind the clipped arch of hornbeam in the southeast corner of my property is the staging ground for the rest of the garden. In this essential but concealed space, newly purchased plants await their placement in the garden, seedlings are sprouted and nurtured, and kitchen and yard wastes are composted. Every plant that goes into the ground spends some time here first.

It is also like a storage closet (and, of course, there is never enough room). When company is coming and time runs short, everything gets shoved back there—tools, equipment, empty pots, wheelbarrows, buckets, bags of mulch, and anything else that looks untidy.

The service yard also affords me a lot of creative space. If I buy plants on impulse and have no idea where they will fit into the garden, I can board them in this service area until I can work it out. It serves as a little nursery for baby plants. On the potting bench in the lathe house seeds are sown, cuttings started, and young and tender plants are encouraged.

BELOW: Fallen leaves and the last splash of floral color accent the narrow stone path of the hallway garden in autumn. The sweet aroma of the silverberry (elaeagnus) hedge fills the air. OPPOSITE: *The hallway garden starts on the south side of my house, as you pass through an arch cut into the Leyland cypress hedge.*

This is also the resting place for material on the way out of the garden. All the leaves, clippings, vegetable peelings, and chicken litter are collected in the compost corrals. Over time, the mixture decomposes and is transformed into rich compost that continues to make my garden flourish. While I try to keep the service yard as neat and attractive as I can, it is the one area of the garden that is more about utility than aesthetics.

The service yard is a slight detour from the main circuit that completely encircles the house. From here the main path continues through the small shade garden and under the clipped hedge arch into a narrow corridor or "hall."

The Hallway Garden

THIS QUIET, NARROW PASSAGEWAY, NOT unlike the halls inside my home, simply serves as a corridor from one room to the next, connecting the shade garden to the front garden where we began our tour. It is enclosed by an elaeagnus hedge on one side and the

colonnade of the porch on the other. In this slender ten-foot space, the stone path that began in the shade garden continues through its center. A pair of trellises supporting white 'New Dawn' roses punctuates a side porch entry to the house. These upright structures help me to use the space more efficiently by lifting plants vertically out of the way of the path. In narrow passages such as this, the shape and form of plants become more important as available space is limited.

The path here narrows, laid only wide enough for visitors to walk single file. The beds to each side of the path are filled with an ongoing and ever-changing flower and design trial. Like other areas of the garden, this is a place where I experiment and observe various combinations of plants. One year the garden hosted only plants in reds and burgundy, a few years later it was transformed into a totally different palette of chartreuse and gray and accented with apricot. At the end of this hall, as you walk under the arching boughs of a pearl bush, you return to the lawn of the front garden, and the circuit is complete.

It has taken me more than ten years to create this garden home from the bare and desolate lot I began with. And even today, it remains a constantly changing and dynamic canvas on which to paint.

Connections

FOR ME, A GARDEN HOME IS much more than just a clever idea; it is a way to make a very real connection to the garden, where I interact with nature every day. The whole purpose for this approach is to lure me out into the garden with rooms that are as comfortable to me as those inside my house.

The rooms in my house fill me with pleasure because they are filled with objects that serve as reminders of my life's journey—everything from photographs and furniture to mementos from family and friends, and even special rocks I've found on meaningful walks. It is a place where I can reflect on the past.

My garden home offers a very different experience; it is a place of constant change. The very nature of the plants and seasons provides a dynamic setting. It is

RIGHT: *Pale yellow foxgloves (*Digitalis lutea*) accent the path. I love the shape of foxglove and make sure their seeds are dispersed in the garden.* OPPOSITE: *In winter, Amaryllis 'Papillon', the stems of red maple (*Acer rubrum*), and paperwhite narcissus bring life to my study.*

where I feel most connected to the present, an area that provides surroundings for personal growth and transformation. Inside, once a chair or a picture is in place, it usually stays there. In my garden home, the seasons, the weather, and daily growth of the plants provide change and surprise, reminding me to live in the present.

The spirit of my garden helps me to withdraw from the lure of the modern world, one seemingly designed to distract me from the deeper parts of myself and my creative nature. The garden can also be a place of ritual. All we have to do is look to the seasons and the rhythms of natural systems to see that the stage for these patterns is already set—winter snows melt into spring's new growth, followed by summer's bounty and autumn's harvest. Connecting to this cadence of the natural home keeps me grounded.

When you look at your garden as an outdoor home, your mind reels with the possibilities of creating comfortable rooms full of vibrant colors, rich textures, patterns, shapes, and forms like those you see inside your home. At the same time, garden rooms set moods that reflect individual style through mystery, surprise, and fun.

As you explore the possibilities of blurring the distinction between the inside and outside of your home, you may begin to look at the interior of your home differently and see ways to bring the outdoors in. For instance, in the autumn, my summer slipcovers come off and interior colors become more earth-tone and warm, vases are filled with fruit laden stems and large bowls spill over with winter squash. Dried blooms of hydrangea, larkspur, and the seed heads of lilies and poppies serve as reminders of the past summer garden, and by January dormant bulbs are emerging from old soup tureens and crocks. In my dining room alone, I fill two large vases with boughs of fiery autumnal leaves until Christmas when they are replaced with greenery. January finds the vases hosting barren winter twigs, and by February they are filled with branches of spring-flowering shrubs. Simply by changing these arrangements through the seasons, the dining room is transformed. By bringing some of the outdoors in, we can become more anchored to a sense of time and place.

THE TWELVE
PRINCIPLES

Enclosure · Shape and Form · Framing the View · Entry ·
Texture, Pattern, and Rhythm

OF DESIGN

Focal Point · Structures · Color · Abundance · Whimsy · Mystery · Time

THROUGH THE YEARS I HAVE HAD THE

GOOD FORTUNE TO CREATE MANY GARDENS ALL OVER THE COUNTRY IN A VARIETY OF CLIMATIC CONDITIONS. SOME HAVE BEEN GRAND AND EXPANSIVE, WHILE others were crafted from the tiniest spaces. I have designed country gardens and gardens in urban settings, gardens for brand-new homes and gardens for older homes in historic neighborhoods. Part of the fun of designing these areas has been that each space was uniquely endowed with its own challenges and attributes.

But despite the variety of these garden experiences, there are essential elements of design that have served me well in fashioning any garden, regardless of its location, size, or growing conditions. These universal principles have become the set of tools I use to create gardens that embody all the key elements of the world's greatest gardens but are scaled to each individual's site, taste, and budget. When woven into the plan of the garden, they are unifying components that magically transform the space into a place of enchantment and beauty. These principles are not ironclad commandments that must be followed to the letter but simply helpful suggestions to assist you as you create the garden of your dreams.

Think of the garden and these principles as a beautiful necklace with twelve precious stones. When seen together, they radiate as one, filling us with wonder and awe. Each stone is exquisite in its own right, but when seen with less than the full complement of twelve, the necklace, while still beautiful, appears less brilliant.

The garden, like the necklace, is most radiant and in harmony when all twelve elements are present. Each one contributes to its overall look. Creating a garden home is about applying these principles in a way that makes a stronger connection between the inside of our homes and our gardens. No doubt nature longs for more association with us, just as we long for nature to be fulfilled in us. A garden home helps us achieve this by creating a life with nature rather than a life apart from her.

The purpose of this section is to define and offer examples of these elements so that you can understand each one before you begin to combine them. They divide naturally into two main categories. The first six—Enclosure, Shape and Form, Framing the View, Entry, Focal Point, and Structures—focus on building the framework or bones of the garden, addressing the "structural" ideas. The second six—Color, Texture, Pattern, and Rhythm, Abundance, Whimsy, Mystery, and Time—add decorative or finishing touches to your garden as well as personality, charm, and—last but not least—fun.

Garden design can be elusive, wily, and even a bit overwhelming, but Mother Nature is ready to meet you halfway. You just have to be willing to take the first steps.

RIGHT: *Spires of foxglove* (Digitalis purpurea) *add height to a wooded perennial garden. The flowers lure the visitor along a path to a distant gate that frames the vista beyond. Here you can see the results of applying several of the twelve principles.*

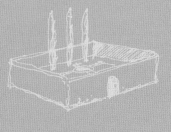

Enclosure

As children we were drawn to secret hiding places, tree houses, and forts where we could meet playmates and create magical adventures. These places of refuge and comfort stirred our imaginations with excitement. In *The Secret Garden*, the classic children's tale by Frances Hodgson Burnett, a world of enchantment and wonder lies hidden away behind the thick walls. Why shouldn't each of us have our own secret garden—not only as a temporary escape from the distractions and demands of everyday life but also as a sanctuary that invites creativity and nurtures the soul? As the saying goes, "Good fences make good neighbors," I have also found that good fences make interesting gardens.

The Art of Containment

THE EARLIEST EXAMPLES OF GARDEN ENCLOSURES, *HORTUS CONCLUSUS*, DATE FROM THE Middle Ages. (The term is Latin: *hortus*, meaning a "garden" or "orchard," and *conclusus*, "closed off.") At that time walled gardens were designed to be places where "nature was tamed by art." But it wasn't until the early twentieth century that the idea of the garden room was fully developed and popularized.

One of the best examples is Hidcote Manor in England. Hidcote's creator, Major Lawrence Johnston, drew on that earlier idea as a basis for the layout, using a series of enclosed rooms as a way to organize and display his vast collection of plants. What Johnston created in 1912 out of an old sheep pasture transformed the way we think of gardens today. His style directly influenced Vita Sackville-West, Russell Page, and many other garden designers throughout the twentieth century. Hidcote is often cited in garden history books for its imaginative plant combinations and use of garden rooms. Here, each enclosure gives way to the next, delighting the visitor at every turn.

Establishing clearly defined enclosures made from a wide selection of materials, including plants, fences, and walls, is a vital element in the design of a garden home. As Johnston found, when rooms have been designed to have their own style and function, it becomes easier to select what goes in each area. Instead of inhibiting your freedom as a gardener, this method actually allows maximum flexibility. Once a framework or "walls" are established, you can, with relative ease, "redecorate" or rearrange the furniture (in this case the perennials, small shrubs, and annuals) as often as you want without remodeling the entire "house."

Enclosures also anchor a garden to its location, giving both the house and the garden a sense of permanence and lasting beauty. They unify house and garden into a cohesive whole, creating a virtually continuous living area.

Since enclosures feel like rooms, the spaces seem familiar to us—areas that have walls, doorways, floors, ceilings, and furnishings. This provides a sense of security, which adds to our comfort and increases the likelihood that we will enjoy using the rooms on a regular basis.

LEFT: *Strong lines provide direction and reassurance. The hedge, boxwood border, white begonias, and the path all repeat the form of this enclosed space.* OPPOSITE: *Like a room with a view, low garden enclosures contain space without constricting the vista beyond. In this front garden, a rose-covered stone wall buffers traffic from a residential street and offers a friendly sense of privacy. Constructed room dividers made from stone, wood, or iron used in combination with plantings create an appealing blend of materials.*

Enclosures can set the stage for a variety of moods and experiences. Tall walls and smaller spaces provide intimate settings while lower borders and larger areas allow for a more open and spacious feeling. By varying the heights of your "walls" and adding "windows," you can create all kinds of imaginative spaces to match the function and style that you select.

I have a clear recollection of a garden I visited as a boy while staying with my grandmother. The house sat smack-dab in the middle of the flat delta plain under a leafy canopy of pecan trees. While the grove offered shade from the

ABOVE: *Symmetry and order reign in this formal enclosure. The formality and scale of the space reflect the grandeur of the large plantation house associated with the garden. The tall, clipped evergreen hedge creates a green room that is intimate and embracing.*

TRELLIS PRIVACY SCREEN

You can divide areas and create a sense of enclosure even in the smallest of spaces. A simple grid trellis anchored in a pair of containers and planted with a quick-growing vine offers an easy solution with beautiful results. This idea is well suited for creating privacy and interest on a patio or roof garden.

STEPS

1. Build trellis.
2. Position terra-cotta pots.
3. Cut PVC sleeves and drainage pipes; insert in pots.
4. Fill pots with concrete to top of drainage pipe.
5. Let concrete set for 48 to 72 hours.
6. Insert trellis support legs into PVC sleeves.
7. Fill with soil and plant with fast-growing vines, such as morning glory or sweet-potato vine.

essential ideas

1. Enclosures are vital elements in defining gardens as rooms.

2. Enclosures anchor a garden to its location, giving both the house and the garden a sense of permanence and lasting beauty.

3. Enclosures unify house and garden into a cohesive whole, creating a virtually continuous living area.

4. Enclosures set the stage for a variety of moods and experiences.

5. Enclosures add a sense of security and comfort by providing familiar structures: walls, floors, doorways, and ceilings.

6. Enclosures establish order by creating manageable-sized spaces.

blazing summer sun and broke up the monotony of the surrounding cropland, it was what lay to one side of the house that captured my attention.

After my grandmother introduced me and my siblings to her friends, Mr. and Mrs. Henegar, we were set free to explore the grounds. The Henegars had created an amazing labyrinth of what seemed at the time like miles of clipped privet hedge gathering beds of flowers and vegetables into colorful bouquets. As I peered into the entry that

led down the mazelike path, I was filled with anticipation. The feeling of suspense, not knowing what I might find around the next corner, was incredibly compelling. Soon I was running through the garden more exhilarated at every turn. It was like tumbling through roofless tunnels that suddenly widened into open rooms—a perfect place for four rambunctious youngsters to play games of hide-and-seek and tag, racing around, shrieking with delight.

The goal of design is to create the best space for living, whether it is inside or out, because in so many ways we not only reflect what surrounds us but also are influenced by the look and feel of our living areas. Each room becomes a place to delight and embrace you, and offers an opportunity to express your personal style. If the enclosures within your garden feel comfortable and inviting, and they are places where you want to be, then you have hit the mark.

ABOVE: *Green holds the garden together. Solid, dark green hedges make excellent backdrops for most plants. In my own garden, 'Annabelle' hydrangea and variegated red twig dogwood would be lost without the visual background provided by the hedge.* OPPOSITE, ABOVE: *Creating a garden home is about making a special place for yourself. Here clematis (C. paniculata) on a trellis, blue Cape leadwort (Plumbago auriculata), and white lantana complete the quiet space for morning coffee.* OPPOSITE, BELOW: *Ornamental grasses (Pennisetum alopecuroides and Calamagrostis acutiflora 'Karl Foerester'), salvia, and lantana create an enclosure. Here I used perennials and annuals to define the enclosed space just until the evergreen framework matures.*

CLOCKWISE, FROM LEFT: *The lines and color of the fence create an architectural extension of this English Tudor house; a flagstone terrace extends the living space of a Victorian home; side gardens frequently offer an opportunity for enclosure; containers and planter boxes form the "walls" of this wooden deck.*
OPPOSITE: *These three columnar Italian cypress trees create the illusion of an enclosed room on this open terrace.*

Shape and Form

SHAPE AND FORM—The contour and three-dimensional qualities of individual plants or groups of plants in the garden, as well as the outline of a garden room itself.

Recognizing basic shapes and geometric forms is a skill developed at an early age. A child's drawing illustrates how objects are symbolized in this simple, straightforward way: a house is drawn as a square or a rectangle, trees are lolli-pops, and people are stick figures with round heads. ❧ As you begin to design your garden, it will serve you well to see the shapes of the plants as if you were looking through the eyes of a child. At first this may seem challenging; our eyes are more accustomed to noticing a plant's flowers, color, or foliage.

But by first identifying a plant's form, you will become skilled at recognizing the role each plays in shaping the look of garden enclosures. In a child's drawing, each shape contributes to the overall composition of the picture. The same is true in your garden. As you add various plants, you begin to set the tone and style for each garden room. I recall the first time I was asked to draw a form without lifting my pencil off the paper—this exercise helped me concentrate on the outline of the object and see its basic contours. A similar exercise might help you visualize the various shapes of plants. The next time you go outside, focus on one plant and try to see it in its simplest form—look past its color and foliage. Identify whether its shape is basically round, oval, oblong, or columnar.

Then recognize the equally important "negative space," or void, around and between plants. This gap is just as much a part of the overall design as the objects themselves. The simpler and more basic the shapes that define this negative space are, the more powerful and memorable it is. For instance, the silhouettes of trees against the sky at dusk are powerful and bold. In the low light the fine details fade and the basic shapes and forms are more clear, allowing you to recognize the importance of basic shapes and how they frame and define negative space.

I recall from my childhood the distinct shapes of oak and cedar trees growing in farmers' fields along the fencerows, standing like cutouts, each with its own personality.

RIGHT: *An archetypal tree, with its distinctive round form silhouetted against an open landscape. Every plant has its own unique shape. Recognizing these can be helpful in the design of the framework of our gardens and the combinations of plants within.*

ABOVE: *Columnar hornbeams (Carpinus betulus 'Fastigiata') provide a stately presence along a narrow terrace near this house. Their distinct shape makes this form an excellent choice for creating a stately pillared addition to the border of this enclosure.* LEFT: *Weeping evergreens like this weeping blue Atlantic cedar (Cedrus atlantica 'Glauca Pendula') make a sensuous accent in the garden when used as a solo specimen.*

Holly (conical)

New Zealand flax (vertical)

PLANT SHAPE	PERSONALITY	EXAMPLES
Columnar	Rigid and regimented; adds formality, order, continuity, elevating effect, draws the eye up	Hornbeam, Italian cypress, arborvitae, fastigiate English oak
Weeping	Flowing, melting, drooping, sad, watery	Willow, weeping forms of cherry, crab apple, cedar, birch, dogwood, redbud; weeping shrubs: cotoneaster, winter jasmine, Virginia sweetspire
Vase	Formal air, lofty and regal	American elm, crape myrtle, burning bush
Fountainesque	Flowing, moving, effervescent, exuberant	Honeysuckle, bridal wreath spirea, forsythia
Vertical and grass-like	Upright, linear, erect	New Zealand flax, agapanthus, iris, upright varieties of ornamental grasses

Boxwood (round—mound)

Weeping willow (weeping)

P L A N T   S H A P E S

Oval	Clearly defined "cotton candy" shape; versatile, depending on setting can be either formal or casual	Flowering pear, sugar maple, London plane tree
Round—mound	At entrances, jolly and fun-loving, neat and friendly	Boxwood, dwarf forms of spirea, conifer, holly, raphiolepis, azalea
Spreading	As wide as its height, comforting, sheltering	Red oak, dogwood, crab apple, cherry, hawthorn
Conical	Stable, grounded, formal	Spruce, pine, cedar, fir, American holly, dwarf Alberta spruce, tulip poplar
Climbing	Casual, uplifting, sometimes wild and unpredictable, romantic	Climbing roses, hydrangea, jasmine, honeysuckle, morning glory, moonflower

Today, in my own garden, in the low evening light, tall, statuesque, columnar English oaks line the street, striking a similar pose to those I remember from my youth.

On another scale, you can experience this same phenomenon when you rearrange the furniture in your home. The look of a room changes and takes on a different feeling as you move your furnishings into new arrangements. Using the same furniture, you can create a traditional, formal arrangement by putting every surface at right angles or a loose, casual layout by placing each piece in a less predictable pattern. While the style of the furnishings influences their arrangement, it is the spatial relationship between the pieces that truly sets the mood.

Positioning shrub and tree combinations in your garden rooms follows the same principles. The individual shape of each plant and how each plant works in combination with others profoundly impact the effect you ultimately achieve. And just as you can identify traditional, modern, or casual furniture styles by their contours, you can associate plant forms with a particular style or look. Columnar, rigid forms bring to mind formal settings, while fountainesque, billowy shapes suggest a more relaxed and informal mode. By understanding the "personalities" often linked with each plant form, you will be better prepared to create plant combinations that will best express the look you have in mind.

ABOVE: *Often a marriage of formal and informal elements works best. Here, a border of boxwood follows the shape of the path, serving to bring order to a bed space full of loose, freely growing roses and perennials.* RIGHT: *The arrangement of shapes and the spaces they create is the foundation of successful garden rooms. This green formal garden is made entirely of clearly defined shapes—spheres, cones, and rectangles.*

SCALLOPED HEDGE

Add flair to your hedge by scalloping the ends. It is easy to do with a template made from a piece of Masonite board.

STEPS
1. Cut out a template.
2. Place the template next to the hedge.
3. Shear the hedge.

The Shape of Garden Rooms

ONCE YOU HAVE AN IDEA OF THE BASIC SHAPES AND FORMS OF INDIVIDUAL PLANTS AND the styles they represent, the next step is to consider how to combine these plants to create the borders of your garden rooms, which will form the walls of your enclosures. To do this, you will need to delineate the outline of the room's shape on the ground. This is an important step. It determines the walls of your garden home and the feeling of the spaces within it.

Selecting a shape to define the boundary of your garden enclosure is the very essence of laying down a solid framework and creating good bones in a garden. Just remember to keep it "simple and natural": Take the simplest form and fit it naturally into the space. Part of the fun of creating a shape for a garden room is that you are not limited to the more traditional square and rectangular rooms found within a home. You can experiment with circles, ovals, and other geometric forms as a part of your design.

The overall shape of a garden room can have symbolic associations. In many cultures, the circle represents infinity because it lacks a beginning and an end. This shape also symbolizes perfection and the eternal. Squares, on the other hand, imply solidity and a certain sense of dependability. Our homes, which are usually square or rectilinear, suggest shelter and safety. The four sides of the square represent wholeness and stand for order in the universe and the balance of opposites. The shape of the cross, found in many cultures, is the intersection at which heaven meets earth: The earth is the horizontal line, and heaven is represented by the vertical.

Combining Plant Shapes and Garden Room Forms

CERTAIN SHAPES AND FORMS SUGGEST A GARDEN ROOM'S STYLE. FORMAL GARDENS ARE GENerally based on principles of geometry and symmetry. Crisp edges, clearly defined lines of demarcation, and ordered patterns appeal to our sense of logic and reason. A medieval knot garden, the simple geometric design of a colonial garden, and the lavish display of a parterre garden seem to satisfy our need for order.

RIGHT: *Effective in both formal and informal settings, the simple lines of a rectangle lend strength and order to any garden room. The vertical blades of* Iris pseudacorus *add a dramatic accent around the bubbling fountain.* OPPOSITE: *A variety of plant forms combine to create a pleasing blend of shapes around this fountain. A large conical holly contrasts nicely with the mounding profusion of 'Fortuniana' roses with the arching branches of* Spirea *'Snowmound' filling the foreground.*

Informal gardens are more relaxed and intuitive, characterized by curved and sinuous lines that appear natural and free-spirited. Plantings are generally less ordered, and their arrangement is not as predictable. In these gardens, nature is allowed to take the lead and man-made interruptions are kept to a minimum.

Visual interest is heightened when these contrasting formal and informal forms are brought together. While shaped hedges might be regarded as a highly formal element, they act as a visual foil to the effusive tumble of perennials, flowering shrubs, and annuals. One client filled a part of her garden with a collection of New England asters, one of her favorite flowers. Even though they bloomed prolifically, the effect seemed too ethereal and undefined. What was lacking were some bold contrasting forms and leaf texture. By simply punctuating the borders with ball-shaped boxwoods, the loose, untamed forms of the borders were transformed, gaining a new sense of order.

I find that many people are drawn to soft and ephemeral plantings of roses, lavender, and baby's breath, which is all fine and good, but without a bold structural framework to support these soft, billowing drifts, the garden somehow falls apart. It is a bit like the concept of yin and yang—wholeness cannot be achieved unless both sides are honored. In Jungian psychology, the analogy would be the anima and the animus—the union of the female and male components in each of us. The softness of the flowers reflects more of the feminine, and the strong outline of the framework responds to the masculine. Both are essential for wholeness and harmony, and the interaction between these opposites animates the design and brings the garden to life.

LEFT: *What may at first seem too formal often softens as a garden matures. I laid out this garden with four equally proportioned rectangular beds, but by late spring the perennials had already obscured the crisp geometric edges.* OPPOSITE: *Rounded forms lend a relaxed feel to a garden room. Here 'Pink Impression' tulips echo the oval shape of this space, blooming under a canopy of four 'Narragansett' crab apples.*

essential ideas

1. Basic shapes stage the look of garden rooms.

2. Shapes have symbolic meanings.

3. Shapes convey "personality" that creates certain moods.

4. The arrangement of shapes in relation to one another defines
    certain styles.

Framing the View

FRAMING THE VIEW — Directing attention to an object or view by screening out surrounding distractions while creating a visually balanced and organized composition.

In gardens, many elements must come together to create beautiful "pictures." Perhaps no principle of garden design fits this art analogy better than that of framing the view. Just as an artist identifies the subject and frames it within the painting, so the garden designer must select and enhance views in a garden by careful framing. One of my favorite things to do when the weather is pleasant is to pack up my easel and art supplies and head out to the country to paint landscapes from life.

One of my tools on such outings is a simple viewfinder, which is nothing more than a rectangular piece of black cardboard with a smaller rectangle cut out of the center. Once I find a site that interests me, I pull out my view-finder to see if any of the surrounding vistas inspire me enough to make them the subject of my painting. If the answer is yes, I hold the viewfinder in place as I make a rough sketch of the composition. Then, as I begin to paint the scene, I periodically check through the viewfinder to keep my composition within the parameters that I initially identified.

This simple act of framing the view helps me focus on the subject and remove surrounding distractions. The same method is useful in the garden. Framing the view means effectively screening and blocking undesirable views or objects to allow you to focus on the most striking components in the landscape.

The scene may be within the garden room or it could be a "borrowed view," such as a vista of a river, a toolshed, a large tree, or even the steeple of a church in the distance. A framed scene could also be a "suggested" view, such as a gate or archway that hints there is something of interest in the adjacent space. While the walls of your garden rooms provide a sense of place and security, a glimpse beyond these boundaries can enlarge the imagination and keep you from feeling confined or claustrophobic.

Framing the view can also be understood from the interior of your home where windows and doors provide views to the outside. These portals "frame" the garden scenes as if they were pictures on the walls of your home.

Axial relationships in your garden also direct the focus within the garden home. A visual axis is the sight line the eye follows to an object or view in the distance. It is guided by screening out distractions surrounding the object or vista, leaving an open "avenue," or clear view toward the subject, such as a terrace or a building at the back of your property.

The primary axis in a garden room is the one that has the strongest vantage point and is directed to the most important object or view in the garden. This sight line can be strengthened even more when the axis begins in the house and continues outside, or goes through more than one garden room, linking them together.

A pleasing framed view is one that feels balanced. It's important to understand that a balanced composition can be either symmetrical or asymmetrical. A symmetrical composition is one that is framed by its mirror image, so on one side of the view you may have a large tree and on the other a matching tree. This is often difficult to achieve in the real world and doesn't necessarily make the most interesting compositions. Rather than reach for symmetry, I ensure that each side of the view has the same visual weight or visual intensity. For example, if a view in a garden has a bank of dark evergreens on the left side, it could be brought into balance if the right side has a cluster of trees or shrubs completely different in shape and form and even color but equal in visual mass. A small building, part of

OPPOSITE: *This classic example of a symmetrical composition at Arley clearly illustrates how a sight line frames the view of the sundial at the terminus of this long vista. While grand in scale, these stately gardens serve as wonderful models for ways to take each principle of design and apply them to your own garden.*

CLOCKWISE, FROM ABOVE: *Rose 'Alchymist' scrambles up and over the archway framing the view into the next garden room; the borrowed view of distant hills becomes part of this garden room's composition with the walkway directing the eye toward the horizon; the balanced symmetry of this arrangement is delicately outlined with a filigree of Boston ivy leaves; twin metal trellises supporting 'Eden' rose contain the garden scene between them.*

CLOCKWISE, FROM LEFT: Diana the Huntress *is seen in a drift of yellow columbine through a framed opening in a hedge; the doors of a study open wide, encouraging frequent visits to the garden; an arc of rose 'New Dawn' enshrouds an angelic fountain; the picket fence and Chinese snowball viburnum* (Viburnum macrocephalum) *layered together create an illusion of screening while affording a view of the garden beyond.*

WINDOW BOX

One easy way to frame a favorite view from a window is to add a window box filled with colorful flowers. Brackets support a 2-by-12-inch board cut to match the window's width. Three holes sized to hold terra-cotta pots allow you to easily change the containers through the season.

STEPS
1. Cut pieces from board.
2. Attach pieces with wood screws.
3. Hang boxes below window.
4. Drop in ten-inch pots. Rims of pots should sit on top of wood.

essential ideas

1. The goal of framing a view is to draw attention to an object or scene.

2. Framing the view can be achieved by opening a sight line to the desired subject and screening out surrounding distractions.

3. Views inside or outside the garden room may be framed.

4. Windows and doorways inside the house serve as frames for outside views.

LEFT: *A rose-covered arbor frames this view into my garden. It is a deliberately composed picture meant to give the passerby a glimpse across the oval lawn.*

your house, or even a piece of sculpture could also bring the composition into balance. Asymmetrical compositions seem to suggest movement. Strict symmetrical compositions, on the other hand, impart a more static, anchored, and fixed feeling to the scene.

The essence of framing the view involves making decisions about what to include and what to exclude from the garden enclosure. Limiting views to a single vista or completely screening out distractions can often pull the space together and make it feel more cohesive and roomlike. Simplicity becomes a powerful device.

Entry

ENTRY—A defined point of entrance into a garden enclosure.

An entry to a garden is often a visitor's first impression. It represents your personal invitation to everything that lies beyond. The allure of an entry is that it is an important point of transition. As the place where people move from the public space into your private world or enclave, the entry sets the mood and style of your garden home. It is another important design element that helps unify your house and garden. ❧ The idea of walking through a door or a gate is fraught with powerful symbolism, and it is an image we see time and again in our culture.

The bride is carried over the proverbial threshold, we enter the "gates" of heaven, and we say, "My door is always open," as a way of offering a standing invitation and an indication of welcome. Clearly this idea of the gate, the door, or the portal provides important imagery that is deeply ingrained in our collective unconscious, so it is important to give careful consideration to this element in your garden.

Have you ever approached a house and been unsure of where you were supposed to enter? You see the front door, but no walkway invites passage and the side door is hidden from view. The garage door looks promising, but you have to weave between cars and boxes to get to it. A well-defined entry is always appreciated by anyone who visits your home.

Welcoming entries should begin well before the porch or front door of the house, when space allows. You can create your own version of a "red carpet," offering family and friends an area where they can feel embraced before they reach the door.

A few signature elements almost always announce "enter here." Piers, gates, and paths, for example, serve as directional guides and are particularly important when the house itself does not make its entry clear. Plants can also help define an entry and more clearly articulate these points of punctuation. A pair of large shrubs at the beginning of a walkway tells the visitor at a glance, "This is the way."

Front and back entries are often given the most attention, but passageways in and out of garden rooms are equally important. As we move from one area to the next,

LEFT: *Over the years this arbor has greeted many friends and visitors to my garden. A rose 'New Dawn' is its carefree companion, making it a picture to behold in May.* OPPOSITE: *Twinkling candlelight adds to the magical feel of entering a private world.*

each point of transition is an opportunity to create a distinctive threshold. These internal entries are also places to build continuity. By repeating some of the same materials or architectural elements from your house in the entries' design, you continue to build on the sense of connection between your home and your garden.

The idea of accenting an entry to our homes is not an abstract or foreign concept. In fact, it is something most of us do every day without even thinking about it. From a doormat that says "Welcome" to pots bursting with seasonal blooms, we are compelled to embellish significant thresholds.

ABOVE LEFT: *A pair of upright massive stones marks the entry to this shady natural garden. A stepping-stone path carries visitors through drifts of fern and native woodland wildflowers.*
RIGHT: *The native scarlet honeysuckle can make an easy-to-grow noninvasive addition to an entry. Its bright tubular flowers entice hummingbirds.*

essential ideas

1. A garden entrance is the first impression of a garden home.

2. Entrances serve as preludes to what lies beyond.

3. Entrances are symbolic signs of welcome.

4. Garden entrances that reflect a home's architectural style create unity.

5. Entrances serve as directional guides and transitional points from one area to the next.

6. Certain key elements serve as components of an entrance.

7. Entries should be a part of each garden room.

PLEACHED ARCH

To create a striking entry, mount a simple grid trellis above a gate. Plant trees with pliable branches suited for pleaching, such as hornbeam, and tie the branches to the trellis.

STEPS

1. Plant one tree on either side of the gate. Allow branches closest to the gate to grow long enough to tie to the trellis.
2. Purchase or build a simple trellis with 6-by-6-inch squares.
3. Mount trellis above gate.
4. Tie longer branches to the trellis with twine.
5. As the tree grows, continue to tie and prune branches.

CLOCKWISE, FROM RIGHT: *I often use a section of fence to conceal the view of a garden and to punctuate its entry; a flowering vine like this Clematis x 'durandii' accents the entrance. This shaded woodland walk gives way to an open clearing filled with light; trees and shrubs can be trimmed to create a natural entrance into an informal garden. These massive wooden gates create a private entrance and signal the style of garden to be found beyond.* OPPOSITE: *An elegant iron gate makes a grand entrance into the walled garden at Arley. The scale and materials herald the richness of the plantings beyond.*

Focal Point

FOCAL POINT—Positioning an object to
draw the eye and to create a feature of attention.

Creating a new garden from "the ground up" is
an opportunity to explore fun ideas and create
spaces ideally suited to the homeowner's needs.
However, refining an existing, mature garden
inspires some of the most creative solutions and
can be just as exciting, while offering the advantage of a garden full of mature plantings. One of
my clients had purchased a great old house with
a neglected garden that was ripe with potential,
but the garden seemed to be missing something.
The crescent-shaped flower beds and old brick
walkways all radiated to a point that begged for
further articulation. Little had been done to the
garden in years; it had escaped and grown wild,
as if nature had come back to claim her own.

LEFT: *This container, filled with sedum 'Vera Jameson', is raised on a stone pier, drawing attention to a change in the garden from one level to the next.* OPPOSITE, ABOVE: *In a small garden, a winding path is interrupted by a circular bed filled with Louisiana iris 'Noble Moment' and an urn on a Doric plinth.* BELOW LEFT: *An urn acts as the focal point in this symmetrical composition, anchoring the scene and commanding attention.* BELOW RIGHT: *In a shady corner, the forced perspective created by the lattice wall adds dimension to the scene and interest to the statue.*

As I snooped around with the new owners behind some overgrown vines, we found a plinth, a square-shaped base for a garden ornament, made of brick about two and a half feet tall. Two broken bolts and a metal ring stain suggested that it had originally been topped with a sundial or an armillary sphere. If this were the case, I thought, to replace it would be a mistake because the scale of the space had changed over time and now the trees and shrubs were mature. The plinth now called for something larger and bolder. Eventually, we found a good-quality reproduction of a handsome urn that was large enough to provide the emphatic punctuation the space demanded.

It is amazing to see how a single object, as the focal point of the garden, can transform the entire area. Once in place, all the other elements seem to come together in harmony. When a single object dominates a space, it has a way of radiating its own energy—almost a center of gravity that anchors and organizes a space. All other objects in the space are measured in some way against it.

ABOVE: *The clock tower at Arley serves as a focal point from many views in the garden, but none so dramatic as this one framed by the double row of pleached lime (Tilia cordata) trees.* RIGHT: *In a smaller space, a client and I chose a statue to subtly punctuate a crescent-shaped pool.* OPPOSITE, LEFT: *Elephant's ear (Alocasia odora) fill an attention-getting blue container.* OPPOSITE, RIGHT: *Don't forget focal points in winter. Here, ice glazes yucca and sedum.*

The Power of Attention

IN A MEMORABLE GARDEN ROOM, A FOCAL POINT SERVES as a visual "hook," a place that catches and holds our interest, making it one of the most powerful elements in design. Focal points can be simple or ordinary objects, such as a bench or a container of flowers to draw the eye. Altering the color of an object by bumping up its intensity or using a shocking hue is another way to create a central focus in a garden.

Perspective also adds power to a focal point, building depth and interest. Trompe l'oeil lattice wall trellises, popularized in the late seventeenth and early eighteenth centuries, are a good example of this element at work in the garden. Lattice slats were simply arranged at slight angles toward an imaginary horizon line, creating the illusion of another layer of dimension. Focal points placed in front of this type of trellis draw the eye to the radiating lines beyond, giving the illusion of an increased depth of field. This is an excellent way to make a small space feel larger, suited to the tiniest terrace or rooftop garden.

Forced perspective can also be applied to the larger landscape,

essential ideas

1. Focal points give space a focus and direction.

2. Focal points visually organize an area.

3. Enhanced perspective adds to the power of focal points.

4. Punctuation is a form of focal points.

91

such as a path leading up to a statue that narrows as it comes closer to the object. In this way, a focal point can serve as a guide, drawing visitors in and directing them toward an object.

With attention focused toward something of interest, the stage is set for the opportunity of surprise. For instance, upon entering a garden room you may see a sculpture in the distance and you are drawn in. Wanting to have a closer look, you walk toward the sculpture but are surprised to discover there are other garden rooms to the right and left. Your curiosity is piqued, encouraging you to explore more of the garden.

ABOVE: *This stone ball, casually placed along the walkway, serves as a punctuation point where two paths come together. It holds visual interest until the 'Clara Curtis' chrysanthemum begins blooming in autumn.*

Punctuation

MUCH LIKE SCULPTURE, PUNCTUATION IS A more understated version of focal point. Examples are clumps of ornamental grass along a path or a grouping of Siberian iris near an entry. Positioned to indicate points of transition in a garden, these objects are simple reminders that a turn is imminent or a passageway will follow. Points of punctuation tend to blend into the fabric of the garden rather than draw attention to themselves as focal points.

In your garden, there should be elements that heighten visitors' curiosity. An essential component in good garden design is to offer visitors a sense of direction and to motivate them to move through a space. When we read a book, even though we do not remember every comma, period, or other punctuation mark that we read, we respond to them subconsciously as they guide us in our interpretation of the information. In much the same way, points of punctuation in a garden can cause us to stop or pause, drawing our attention and enriching our experience of the space.

STRIKING TUTEUR

Fashion an instant focal point with three prefabricated V-shaped trellises and a ball finial purchased at your local home-improvement store.

STEPS

1. Fit together three V-shaped prefab trellises with point ends up.
2. Trim the ends or feet of the trellises so that the tuteur will stand evenly.
3. Paint the trellises.
4. Tie together the prefab trellises with copper wire.
5. Cut a circular piece of wood as a base for the finial to sit on. The diameter of the circular piece should match the diameter of the foot of the finial. The prefab finials will have a screw that drops down from the bottom. Drill a hole into the center of your circular base and screw the finial into the circular base.
6. Paint the finial and base.
7. Nail the circular base and finial to the top of the tuteur.

Structures

STRUCTURES—A variety of constructed features within the garden.

A hallmark of grand gardens is the skillful integration of garden structures that seamlessly blend into the overall design. Because the combination is so flawless, both the garden and the structure are enhanced. This effect can be achieved on a more modest and realistic scale in our own household gardens. ❧ From an early age, I learned the value of taking a sow's ear and turning it into a silk purse. This lesson of frugality and resourcefulness came from both my mother's and my father's sides of the family. Slipcovers transformed tired, old chairs, and painted furniture freshened rooms without great expense.

Seeing the virtue in what we had and learning how to make the most of it is an approach I have since applied to my garden designs. There is something exhilarating about embellishing an ordinary outbuilding to make it more attractive and then integrating it into the framework of a garden. Out of practical and sometimes mundane objects, we can create beauty.

This is particularly true in small gardens when buildings become part of the framework. With proper planning and some creativity, these structures can serve both functional and aesthetic purposes instead of becoming eyesores. They can add to the sense of enclosure, screen views, and provide a center of visual interest while also satisfying practical needs. Enhance commonplace buildings with bits of trellis, for example, or cover an unsightly roof in climbing roses. The results can transform the space. These garden "slipcovers" are easy and affordable ways to balance the longing for beauty with the realities of a limited budget or a lack of space.

Structures such as new or remodeled buildings, arbors, trelliage, and simple supports for plants play an important role in a garden's framework. They represent an anchoring element, a firm point from which we can begin to absorb the richness and diversity of the entire space. In the garden home, structures articulate the transition between the house and the garden, often becoming a bridge between these two worlds.

The Japanese have expanded this idea of combining the inanimate and living elements in the way they interpret their landscapes. In their gardens, large stones represent the female side of the garden, constant and never changing. They are stationary and grounded to the earth, in direct contrast to the ever-changing plants, which represent the male spirit—always transforming and fickle.

LEFT: *Structures can serve as transition from home to garden. Here rose 'Buff Beauty' is supported by the heavy timbers and rustic stone columns of this handsome pergola.* OPPOSITE, ABOVE: *The finishing touch of this strong and distinctive roof is a copper cupola. Finials, weather vanes, and cupolas all add personality and charm to garden structures.* OPPOSITE, BELOW: *Rose 'Eden' has been trained to a simple metal frame to create a more substantial structure.*

essential ideas

1. Structures serve both functional and aesthetic purposes.

2. Structures add to the sense of enclosure, screen views, and provide a center of visual interest.

3. Structures represent an anchoring element, a firm point from which we can begin to absorb the richness and diversity of the entire space.

4. Structures articulate the transition between house and garden.

FAR LEFT: *Expressing personal style, these gourds growing from a long arbor create a fun and almost surreal landscape in late summer.* LEFT: *A metal frame anchored into the brick wall supports the wisteria, allowing it to grow the entire length of the house.* OPPOSITE: *A private enclosed space, as seen from a bedroom of the house to which it belongs, was created by integrating the stone toolshed and adjacent walls into the plan. Thornless and evergreen 'Lady Banks' rose provides an exuberant display of bloom in early spring.*

The combination of these two contrasting elements makes Japanese gardens more compelling and dynamic and gives them soul. Your garden structures serve as similar contrast to your flowers and foliage.

Structures in all their various forms and functions have always been a part of the American garden scene. Architect and lifelong gardener Thomas Jefferson sketched plans for more than twenty garden structures to be used throughout the landscape at his home, Monticello. They played an important role in his garden design and in the landscape he spent much of his adult life improving. The best contemporary structures are those that not only serve a number of uses, offering both beauty and function, but also are well integrated into the garden plan.

One of the best examples of the perfect blend between structures and garden can be found at Sissinghurst Castle, a National Trust garden in Kent, England. There, Harold Nicolson and Vita Sackville-West used the remains of an Elizabethan manor as a point of departure for creating a garden commonly regarded as a twentieth-century masterpiece. Harold's interest lay in the buildings and framework of the garden; Vita brought a passion for plants and plant combinations. Together, they created just the right mixture of both: a garden that continues to inspire all who experience it.

GARDEN STRUCTURES CAN TAKE MANY FORMS

Porches
Loggias
Pergolas
Summerhouses
Gazebos
Cabanas
Belvederes
Decks
Terraces
Patios
Follies
Treehouses

STRUCTURES OF UTILITY
Toolshed
Potting shed
Storage buildings
Chicken house or doghouse
Raised beds
Compost bin

SUPPORTS FOR PLANTS
Arbors
Bowers
Trellises
Tuteurs
Planter boxes

CREATING A TRELLIS

A trellis adds dimension to your garden's framework, giving an outdoor room more interest. A simple grid pattern is a classic style, blending with most garden motifs. Use copper sleeves to create space between the trellis and the wall. This allows air to circulate around the plant and is less damaging to the wall's surface.

STEPS

1. Measure for trellis dimensions.
2. Cut weather-resistant boards to size.
3. Glue and nail the boards together.
4. Cut lengths of copper pipe.
5. Attach to wall with wood screws and washers, using copper pipe segments as spacers.

CLOCKWISE, FROM LEFT: *The lax stems of vines and climbers, such as this evergreen* Clematis armandii, *receive support as they reach for the light; the salmon-colored blooms of rose 'Abraham Derby' are in concert with the warm ocher tones and ivy-covered portico of the stone house; rose 'New Dawn' spills over the corner of my garage, creating a wall of fragrance to the loggia; rose 'Lamarque' is festooned over the entry to my toolshed, which is also the shelter for my chickens and an important focal point.*

Color

COLOR—Orchestrating the color palette in the garden through the selection and arrangement of plants and objects.

How to use color in the garden effectively is, for most of us, an elusive and mysterious concept that can at times be intimidating, but once understood, it is exciting and rewarding. Of course, we all have our favorite colors, and certainly color has plenty of cultural associations. Pink is for girls, blue is for boys; white knights are the good guys; orange means caution, red means stop. The list goes on. We are already accustomed to thinking about color; all that is left is to see how it improves the garden and how we can use it to achieve the desired effect.

Ask three people to describe the color of a room or an object and more often than not you will get three different descriptions. Color is subjective, and how we respond to it depends on several factors—our individual backgrounds, the context in which the color is seen, and most important, the light. Without light there is no color. Light is essential not only for life but for the way in which color is perceived. In addition, we have to allow for light and shadow and how all of these factors change with the weather and time.

As a self-taught artist, I have come to understand color the hard way, through trial and error, by creating my own share of bad paintings. But often my failed experiments have been my best teachers. The lesson that took the longest to learn was to be bold and generous with color in the garden as well as on the canvas. Broad sweeps of color, with one shade diffusing into the next, were much more effective than a few dots and splashes here and there.

Gardeners develop their own rules of thumb for using color. One I have come to rely on is to create a green framework that holds the garden together. Shades of green in a garden serve as a frame, just as wall color in an interior room provides a unifying

ABOVE: *The intensity of the contrasting hues of the bright yellow coreopsis 'Sunburst' and rich blooms of purple statice provides a bold accent.* LEFT: *A simple set of watercolors has always served as a useful device for me in working through color combinations. From bold to subtle, hot to cool, a rainbow of color can be found in the blooms and foliage of plants.* OPPOSITE, ABOVE: *The clear pink color of this drift of surprise lilies* (Lycoris squamigera) *resonates with the color of the house.* BELOW LEFT: *Thrift* (Phlox subulata) *bursts into brilliant waves of color in spring.* BELOW RIGHT: *A combination of three varieties of pink petunias planted en masse is more interesting than a single shade.*

CLOCKWISE, FROM ABOVE: *The globe-shaped blooms of* Echinops bannaticus *'Taplow Blue' dance atop gray foliage. The mauve crepe-like blooms of this poppy (*Papaver somniferum*) are a beautiful accent among white roses. The blue-gray leaves of hosta 'Krossa Regale' evoke a cool, calm feeling. The bright blue blooms of spiderwort (*Tradescantia*) blend with the intensely fragrant magenta flowers of rose 'Russell's Cottage' as variegated Solomon's seal (*Polygonatum odoratum *'Variegatum') fills the foreground. The buds of common morning glory unfurl into trumpets of color that range from vibrant pinks to purples.*

CLOCKWISE, FROM ABOVE: *Asiatic lily 'Enchantment' is a reliable source of intensely rich orange color. The dark, somewhat somber façade of this house provides the perfect background for the tulip 'Menton'; the success of this color combination lies in the fact that red is present in both the mellow salmon pink of the tulip and the brown of the house. Bright and unapologetic orange marigolds make their presence known in the garden. The soft apricot color of this Aurelian hybrid lily 'Golden Splendor' exhibits the gentler side of orange. The cheerful, clear yellow of a forsythia shrub's blooms is the perfect companion to spring daffodils.*

essential ideas

1. A green framework holds the garden together and serves as a background for other colors.

2. Colors create moods and illusions.

3. The intensity of light affects color.

4. Use no more than one color theme for each garden room. Greens and grays act as harmonizers between contrasting colors.

5. A garden's color scheme should match the house and other outstanding features.

6. Growing conditions of gardens may limit color schemes.

7. Broad sweeps of color are more effective than dabs and patches.

element for the other colors in the room's furniture, draperies, and accessories. The greens of hedges and shrubs offer a harmonizing background for the disparate elements in a garden room and a respite for the eye between color schemes.

Another guideline I have found useful is to match the mood of the room with colors that evoke that feeling. Cool colors such as blue and lavender soothe, helping us to feel restful and

ABOVE LEFT: *A spray of rose 'Old Blush' cascades over the fence in early spring. The deep pink buds of this reliable bloomer open to a lighter pastel shade.* ABOVE: *A brilliant stand of Mexican sage* (Salvia leucantha) *makes a dramatic show in the late-summer garden.* OPPOSITE: *The pastel hues of dianthus 'Bath's Pink' and rose 'Perle d'Or' are in concert with the emerging gray foliage of Russian sage.*

RIGHT: *The hues of roses 'Caldwell Pink',* *'New Dawn', and 'White Pet' work* *together.* OPPOSITE, ABOVE: *Crocosmia* *'Lucifer' electrifies the herbaceous borders* *at Arley.* BELOW LEFT: *Annuals such as* *Flanders poppies can bring a splash of red* *into the garden. The short-lived flowers* *will produce thousands of seeds for next* *year's bloom.* BELOW RIGHT: *The fiery* *red-orange blooms of this Turkscap lily* (Lilium martagon) *add a spark to even* *semi-shady areas in the garden.*

calm, while hot colors such as reds and oranges stir warmth and excitement, simulating the urgency of fire and blood. Broad sweeps of these colors add an emotional charge to your garden rooms. Consider, too, that colors create illusions of space. Like the blue sky, cool colors give the feeling of distance, while hot colors appear closer.

It is important to remember that colors are not viewed in isolation but in association with the other colors around them. Garden designers take in the whole palette of colors in the surrounding areas to create harmonizing combinations. Buildings and outstanding features within the garden, such as a flowering tree or a garden ornament, can all be points from which a color scheme is developed. When a room in the house opens directly into a garden enclosure, an opportunity to extend a color theme from one realm into the next presents itself. When choosing flowers for cutting, consider the impact your color selections from the garden will have on the color of your home's interior.

Another important rule for using color effectively is to limit your selections in each garden room to the range of a single color family, with perhaps a bit of its complement for contrast. Don't use too much. Each enclosure should have its own color theme, just like each room of your house. A garden room can be simple and monochromatic, or it can have a well-coordinated range of colors with just a splash of contrast to invigorate the feeling of space.

CLOCKWISE, FROM LEFT: *The pale purple color of lavender 'Provence' flowers is echoed in the underplanting of red cabbage and blue pansies. The metallic-like quality of sea holly (*Eryngium maritimum*) glistens among other perennials and blends with a variety of color schemes. The soft powdery blue of* Plumbago auriculata *or* Cape leadwort *creates a cool effect in areas where the summers can sizzle. Ice-blue blooms of delphinium 'Blue Elf' lend a sense of tranquillity to almost any setting; this shade of blue seems to be universally compatible with every other color in my garden. In this composition, serene blues in the form of agapanthus and salvia 'Indigo Spires' harmonize with the frosty gray of the sea holly.*

CLOCKWISE, FROM FAR LEFT: *Variegated winter creeper is an evergreen groundcover that brightens dark shady areas of the garden. The long, tubular blooms of flowering tobacco (Nicotiana sylvestris) fill my garden with an intoxicating fragrance and glistens in the early evening light. Cool greens harmonize with the weathered hues of an old stone wall while the crisp white 'Iceberg' roses freshen the composition. This chartreuse coleus carries a tangy brightness in its foliage, a good contrast to other greens, salmons, oranges, and purples. The pure white of clematis 'Candide' is refreshing in the spring garden and a perfect complement to old-fashioned shrub roses and climbers.*

MADE-TO-ORDER DAYLILIES

If you are unable to find the right daylily for your garden's palette, why not create your own? Daylilies are easy to hybridize, and you can see the results in just a few seasons.

STEPS:

1. Select parent daylilies.
2. Collect pollen from daylily A and apply to daylily B.
3. Label daylily B for future reference.
4. Once daylily B has flowered and formed a seedpod that opens, collect seeds that are black, shiny, and plump.
5. Store the seeds in an airtight freezer bag in the refrigerator for 6 to 8 weeks.
6. Sow the seeds.
7. Transplant seedlings to selected locations.

In the garden, green is not only the predominant color but also the neutral, much as beige or taupe is in our home interiors. When you choose colors of plants and accessories, keep in mind that they will be viewed against this backdrop of green and consider the relationship of their colors. You can interrupt areas of intense color with sections of green or use gray foliage plants to synchronize areas of conflicting color. Another option is to design the garden room so that the color palettes change seasonally—spring pastels give way to warmer colors in the summer.

Color is a compelling and exciting element of design when used as a means of self-expression. We articulate these preferences in our clothes, cars, and interior design. Color in the garden should be equally expressive and personal. Experiment with color in a way that will make your heart and garden sing.

ABOVE: *Seasonal bouquets of cut flowers are a good way to experiment with color combinations for the garden. Here orange and a range of pinks create a vibrant and festive display.*

Texture, Pattern, and Rhythm

TEXTURE, PATTERN, AND RHYTHM—Using surface characteristics, recognizable motifs, and the cadence created by the spacing of objects as elements of design.

The beauty of flowers has seduced us all. Who hasn't been to a garden center in the spring and been swept into a buying frenzy, giving little thought to where the flowers in bloom will be planted or what the foliage will look like after the flowers fade? Well, a plant's foliage is just as important, if not more so, than its blooms. The reality is that most trees, shrubs, and perennials make a bold showing of flowers for a few weeks each summer, and we spend the rest of the year staring at their branches and leaves.

Mother Nature is very clever this way. First she attracts us with her flowers. Over time, as we become better acquainted, we begin to recognize other aspects of plants that are as interesting as the blooms. Being aware that there is more to a garden than colorful flowers is an important realization.

Imagine that we lived in a world without color. What would be visually exciting in our gardens? Even in the absence of color we can count on texture, pattern, and rhythm to contribute richness and interest. Some of the most beautiful and satisfying gardens are green foliage gardens that depend almost entirely on their framework and textural contrast to create enchanted spaces. When complementary textures are juxtaposed with one another, the intensity of each is heightened, just as we find with color. Without the richness of texture, pattern, and rhythm, our gardens would be flat and vapid and would fail to inspire and excite us.

Texture

TO USE TEXTURE SUCCESSFULLY IN YOUR GARDEN, YOU NEED TO TRAIN YOUR EYE TO REC-ognize it. For instance, the first step is observing how dark, glossy leaves reflect light and soft fuzzy plants absorb it.

The next step is to begin contrasting these different textures, one against the other. The more extreme the contrast, the more aware we become of the individual qualities of each participant. Flowers offer as much textural diversity as foliage. Some are light, airy, and translucent, while others can be bold, flashy, opaque masses of color. Contrasting bloom shapes and textures is an important key to more artful compositions in the garden. If we view

flowers as simply another form of texture to add to our palette, then we can put them in proper perspective and see them as "icing on the cake" instead of the only reason to use a plant.

The texture of plants can also transport us to another place. Foliage plants with large bold leaves, such as magnolias, cannas, and castor beans, evoke the

RIGHT: *Water beads glisten on the fuzzy foliage of stachys 'Helen von Stein'.* OPPOSITE, ABOVE: *A green tapestry is accented with lavender from* Hydrangea villosa, *but it is foliage texture that gives this bog garden visual appeal.* BELOW LEFT: *Graceful and old-fashioned, this hedge of spirea creates a loose, frothy texture when covered with these miniature bouquets of white flowers.* BELOW RIGHT: *I use the contrasting textures of hostas and ferns as a classic combination for shade.*

semitropics. Likewise, the thick, leathery, and often spiny foliage of succulents, cacti, and yucca reminds us of the desert.

Building materials offer their own textures and colors, establishing an important dynamic between the two realms—the static and the living. Just as the color of your house influences the palettes you choose for plant combinations, you should consider the texture of your house as well. Bold foliage against smooth stucco, or delicate, lacy leaves contrasted with rough, coarse stone, makes full use of texture in the garden, as each surface flatters the other.

Texture can alter our perception of distance and sense of perspective in our gardens. Tightly clipped, dense plants that are dark green in color, such as boxwoods, hollies, and laurels, make a space appear smaller because they lack any transparency or depth. Lighter-colored and looser foliage plants used as the borders of a garden space can make the same area feel larger because we can see into and through them. Deciduous shrubs such as spirea, rugosa roses, and hornbeam foster this effect.

The same principle is true when arranging your flower beds. By placing a plant with a bold texture in front of

ABOVE: 'Spring Green' tulips pick up the detail of the porch banister. OPPOSITE: A small planting of golden Diosma (breath of heaven) illuminates the edge of a shady grove. The silhouette pattern of tree trunks in the distance adds to the composition.

one with a finer texture, you can create an illusion of depth, since bold-textured foliage appears to be closer, while fine textures appear farther away. Plants with large distinctive leaves provide an immediate focus for the eye, jumping forward rather than receding into accompanying foliage, while those with fine texture and an airy habit have a transparent quality, particularly when used at the front of a border or bed. Their delicate stems and leaves create a screen through which other plants can be seen. Peruvian verbena, gaura, angels'-fishing-rods (*Dierama*), Russian sage (*Perovskia*), and ornamental grasses rank among the best for creating this effect.

Just as the color blue creates the illusion of greater distance in the garden, the silhouettes of trees with ephemeral canopies blend with the sky to achieve the same feeling. Movement and changing light bring life to the garden. The dance of dappled shade on a lawn or walk at midday or the gradual dominance of darkness as the sun lowers into the horizon is a part of an ever-changing landscape. The texture of the plants we use contributes to these effects. Trees with large, coarse-textured leaves and open canopies will create a more interesting interplay of light and shadow in the garden than trees with smaller leaves and a denser habit.

Large stretches of a single plant or group of plantings can help us employ texture on a more expansive scale, so

CLOCKWISE, FROM ABOVE: *The refined stems and flowers of guara add a delicate and airy feeling to the flower border and allow us to see other plants through it; as the inflorescence of purple fountain grass moves with the breeze, it contrasts with the broad and bold canna leaf; variegated grasses such as ribbon grass (Phalaris arundinacea) are an easy way to add pattern to the garden; upon close inspection, the leaf of this smooth-veined canna ('Black Knight') reveals its own internal texture, pattern, and rhythm.*

CLOCKWISE, FROM ABOVE: *The variations in color and pattern of the bark on this plane tree* (Platanus occidentalis) *will become more pronounced as it ages. Because of their varying leaf shapes, succulents such as this dudleya are a rich source of texture, whether planted directly in the garden or in a container. The foliage and bloom of 'Marie Pavie' roses are a nice contrast to the blue-gray leaves of hosta 'Krossa Regale'. The plumelike blooms of astilbe 'Peach Blossom' offer a soft and friendly texture in late spring, and because they thrive in moist, humus-rich soil, they make good companion plants for hosta, spiderwort, and ferns.*

don't underestimate the importance of a lawn as a source of texture in the garden. The smooth carpetlike texture of mowed grass is a visual foil for the foliage plants on the periphery. The predominant use of one plant or texture creates a basis against which other things are measured. We begin to see everything else as bolder than, coarser than, more refined than this principal texture. This is particularly effective in small gardens. An occasional flowering tobacco with its broad, bold leaf helps to offset myriad refined blooms of lantana, gaura, and verbena.

Pattern

PATTERNS ARE AN INTEGRAL PART OF THE NATURAL WORLD AND OUR GARDENS. SOME OF the most exciting motifs are derived from nature, each unique and wondrous. The veining in a leaf, the arrangement of bark on a tree, and the scales on a butterfly's wing are but a few of the endless examples of patterns found in nature. Weaving these varied designs into the fabric of our garden rooms adds depth and character.

Leaves patterned with areas of light and dark appear to be dappled in sunlight. Variegated patterns found in certain foliage provide lightness and movement to darker areas of the garden. Golden- and chartreuse-colored plants appear sun kissed, bringing a shine to areas that need some sparkle.

STONE MOSAIC ENTRY PAD

Add pattern, texture, and rhythm to your garden with an entry pad mosaic made of cut stone, bricks, and river rock.

STEPS

1. Dig out the space where the entry pad is to go.
2. Insert two-by-four lumber around the edges of the space to hold the concrete.
3. Pour the concrete and level to create the pad. Allow to set overnight.
4. Place and grout the edging stones.
5. Place and grout the bricks.
6. Allow the bricks and edging stones to set overnight.
7. Fill in the remaining space with grout and set the river rock.

When repeated, patterns and motifs create a continuum within a garden room. Use paths, fences, trellises, and structures as reoccurring themes that give harmony to the design. Plants, too, can make thematic contributions. My romance with old-fashioned roses is a theme that can be followed through each of the rooms of my garden home, and is never more apparent than during that magical moment in May when all the roses bloom at once.

Rhythm

RHYTHM IS AN IMPORTANT EXTENSION OF PATTERN. THE REGULAR PLACEMENT OF OBJECTS establishes a cadence that plays an active role in the character development of a garden room. Just as we establish a rhythmic stride when walking on stepping-stones along a path, several objects equally spaced in an obvious pattern can create a visual beat. Trees in a row, a series of containers, groups of plants, drifts of flowers, or bold splashes of color and texture set a rhythm that implies order and dependability. The relationship between objects in the landscape communicates rhythm. Both the objects themselves and the "empty" spaces between them create these dynamic recurring beats.

How many elements does it require to create a rhythm? Three or more distinct, successive objects are needed. The bolder they are, the more aware we become of their influence on us. These repeating forms establish a visual

pace that can affect the way we move through our gardens and how we perceive them. Once we pick up on the rhythms, we begin to recognize everything else in relation to these points of punctuation; a sense of order or logic is created that is reassuring due to its predictability. Repeated objects placed closely

LEFT: *Simple geometric patterns can make a bold mark in the garden. A bed of ageratum, punctuated by gumdrop-shaped* Chamaecyparis pisifera *'Boulevard', surrounds the fish boy fountain at Arley.* OPPOSITE: *A row of Italian cypress lends a stately air as they create a sense of rhythm and order along the balustrade of this formal terrace. I added rose 'Alister Stella Gray' and yaupon holly to help anchor the composition.*

together tend to quicken the rhythm, and the same objects spaced farther apart slow it down. When placing a series of objects, remember that their spacing helps to suggest the pace of the rhythm. It has a psychological effect on our movement through the space. For example, the spacing of columnar evergreens along a path may influence your stride as you walk down that path. Long stretches between each tree invite a more relaxed and leisurely walk, while arranging them closer to one another might encourage you to quicken the pace.

Undulating and sinuous lines also create rhythm and movement in the garden. The soft, regular curves of a serpentine line imply fluidity and have a relaxing effect. Narrow paths that wind and meander require more of our attention and time to stay on course, thus slowing us down. On the other hand, we can move quickly down a wider, more generous linear path.

When included in the garden's framework, texture, pattern, and rhythm make enormous contributions to the visual appeal and mood of a garden. They set the mood, which can be calming and restful, encouraging us to lounge and relax, or dynamic and vibrant, inspiring us to explore and move about. We use these elements to create gardens that provide year-round appeal, where flowers act as seasonal highlights.

essential ideas

1. Texture, pattern, and rhythm add layers of richness and interest to a garden.

2. Contrasting surface characteristics of plants and materials heighten the visual impact in garden rooms.

3. Repeating motifs create a continuum within a garden room and give harmony to the design.

4. The cadence created when three or more objects are equally spaced in an obvious pattern set a rhythm that implies order and dependability.

5. Repeated objects placed closely together tend to quicken the rhythm, and the same objects spaced farther apart slow it down.

ABOVE: *Creating rhythm by altering the shape of hedges is a way to establish a consistent pattern in the garden. To add a level of visual interest in this small urban garden, I crenellated a low boxwood hedge.* OPPOSITE: *Here I used a serpentine border of boxwood to create a rhythm along a garden pathway.*

Abundance

ABUNDANCE—An ample to overflowing quality created by the generous use of plants and materials.

There are moments in our lives when we see, often quite suddenly, our familiar and ordinary world in a completely different way. These moments can be as profound as they are unexpected. ❧ One summer day, when walking with a friend of mine in a new garden I had helped her and her husband design, we were both transfixed by its transformation. It had grown with utter abandon since the last time I had seen it. Despite its newness—the garden was then only two years old—it was full and vibrant: the young perennials were already making clumps, the shrubs were settling in, full and robust, and the annuals planted just that season filled in with a riotous display.

As we walked past the drifts of ornamental grasses waving in the wind and mounds of purple sage, we found its beauty disorienting; it distracted us from our conversation and finally we had to stop and be still as we looked on in wonder.

After a long pause, my friend broke the silence: "When we are in the presence of the divine, we can feel the abundance. We are fed in so many ways by being around this kind of bounty." And there, in that moment, gazing at the fullness of what that small space had produced, I recognized the presence of the divine. This was a place where the cup was not just half full, but brimming over with abundance. It represented, in very real terms, the life force, inviting us to connect to it each day.

Nature's Lessons

GARDENS ARE ABOUT MAKING BOLD STATE-ments. The credit for this idea goes to Mother Nature. As you look around natural settings, you will find that plants often grow in large colonies. If you follow this lead, then your garden will appear more spontaneous and natural. Isolated pockets of plants seem artificial and contrived. A more relaxed planting style, where plants are arranged in groupings of three, five, or seven, is generally more pleasing to our eye than plants lined rigidly along the edge of a bed or a lawn.

That's not to say that you should pack all the plantings together. The groupings should have some room between them, as well as at the edge of the border, wall, or house. Crowding plants together without some visual space in between gives the area a congested, forced look. Remember, plants will grow, so give them plenty of room to reach their potential. Often, when you consider their mature size, you won't need to space them as closely as you might think, so instead consider planting them in larger, more effective drifts.

Invariably, when I advise people to be generous with their plantings, they ask, "How will I know when I've planted too much?" They wonder if there is a difference between abundance and excess. The answer is yes. Excess is when a single element dominates a composition to the point of becoming a distraction, overtaking the other design elements. Abundance has to be contained to gain its full effect. We live in an age when the operative message seems to be "too much is just enough." But in the garden, like life itself, such unbridled excess rarely satisfies.

ABOVE: *This rich combination of 'Menton', 'Temple of Beauty', and 'Perestroyka' tulips makes such a bold impression, the memory of this display will linger throughout the year.*
LEFT: *Nature can help us with our plant selections. By observing how plants prosper in their native environs, we can apply them better in our own gardens. These ferns have colonized along a cool and damp bank.*
OPPOSITE: *Daffodil 'Ice Follies' is one of my favorites. It is a reliable and generous multiplier. Here bold drifts brighten a somber wood in March.*

One way to avoid excess is to use a handful of plant varieties to make up the bones or framework of a garden. Over the years, I have created a stable of "workhorse" plants that I use generously throughout the garden. To qualify, they must be hardy, pest-free, and reliable—and, of course, I have to like them. Italian gardens, in all their elaboration and glory, are for the most part made up of surprisingly few plants—cypress, laurel, boxwood, oak, and citrus often dominate. The bones of my own garden rely on crab apple, holly, boxwood, and old-fashioned shrub roses. The remainder of the plants fill in and harmonize with the framework. Identify your own growing area's "workhorse" plants. Keep the selection simple and use them over and over again, then add variety with the accent plantings.

Another way to fill your garden with abundance is to plant enough flowers to pick and enjoy indoors without feeling like you have visually weakened the strength of the display. For example, I always pack in extra tulip and

daffodil bulbs to the drifts I plant so when I cut them for spring bouquets, I haven't destroyed their overall effect. Another trick is to plant equal numbers of early, middle, and late spring bloomers. By choosing varieties with different bloom times, you extend the impact of the display while maximizing the use of the bed space. This technique will help you enjoy the flowers in waves of color.

One of the blessings of abundance is having enough to share with others. Some gardeners love to offer their vegetables to neighbors; others plant a row for the hungry and give their surplus crops to local shelters. In both cases the reward of

LEFT: *Nature is the most generous gardener. Larkspur, when allowed to reseed, will return year after year with little or no effort.* OPPOSITE: *The fundamental geometry of my garden provides a framework so that the garden's abundance never appears to be chaotic.*

BOUNTIFUL HYDRANGEAS

One of the joys of gardening is the ability to increase certain plants through cuttings. Hydrangeas are one of the easiest plants to propagate this way.

STEPS
1. Take cuttings from the parent plant.
2. Strip the lowest pair of leaves.
3. Wet ends and dip in rooting powder.
4. Stick into a container of moist soil
5. Keep the soil consistently moist.
6. Transplant in six to eight weeks.

sharing makes the extra effort spent planting seem worthwhile.

Giving friends and family your favorite "pass-along plants," those that have been handed down from one gardener to the next, is another way to be generous. The plants carry with them a sense of history, place, and nostalgia. One of my gardening friends was always very generous with the daylilies and iris he hybridized, as well as his favorite daffodil bulbs. He gave them to many of his friends and several gardening organizations. Now that he has passed away, his plant gifts shine in gardens throughout the city. As he shared the gifts from his garden, he left a legacy of his work, inspiring others to do the same.

Sharing the bounty of the garden is one of the greatest joys of having one. By their very nature they are places of abundance. The gardener who plants with a generous spirit is always amply rewarded.

ABOVE: *Bold clumps and drifts in defined groups bring order to this curved border of perennials and shrubs. Generous masses of Siberian iris, alliums, and roses fill the beds with seasonal blooms without feeling crowded.*

essential ideas

1. Plants growing in a large drift or colonies appear spontaneous and natural.

2. To gain its full effect, abundance has to be contained to the point where it is not a distraction.

3. A few "workhorse plants" used generously establish abundance without excess.

4. Generous plantings allow selective cuttings without diminishing the overall visual impact.

5. Staggered bloom times extend the impact of the display while maximizing the use of the bed space.

6. Ample plantings provide enough to share.

Whimsy

WHIMSY—Elements of lighthearted fancy.

Life in general and gardens in particular are much more enjoyable with a sense of humor. Once, on a trip to Italy, my hosts insisted that I walk alone through a garden in a villa we were visiting. As I ventured out, I descended into a series of chambers that eventually led me onto an elaborate sunken parterre. I became suspicious when they sent me ahead, saying they would wait for me at a lookout above. Even though I sensed something was up, I went on, cautiously exploring the narrow cavelike walls, when suddenly a jet of water shot up from the floor, then another from the side. I jolted forward, only to have another squirt me in the face.

Each step was matched with a spray of water that continued until I made my way out and onto the parterre, where my friends were now howling with laughter. Standing there soaked, I realized I had just been introduced to the *giochi d'acqua*, or the water joke—humor, Italian Renaissance–style.

Such devices, designed to entertain guests, were fairly common in the grand Italian gardens and the one at the Villa Torrigiani was, after four hundred years, still in fine working order! Most gardening cultures have some sense of fun: The Italians have their jokes, silly sculptures, and playful grottoes studded with seashells; the English have follies shaped like pineapples and castle ruins; and the Americans have pinwheels and gnomes.

A touch of whimsy is an element I try to incorporate in all of my garden designs. It works best when it relates to the personality of the owner. For example, I once suggested to a friend who was a great lover of Sir Walter Scott's nineteenth-century romantic tales that the pond behind his house would be a perfect place to add a sword rising from the surface, creating his very own *Lady of the Lake*. To another friend, who had a houseful of exceptionally "quotable" children, I proposed that we immortalize some of their most humorous statements by engraving them into stepping-stones for her garden.

The names of plants can also bring delight to the garden home and a smile to our faces. Old-fashioned names like "cat's whiskers," "Johnny jump-ups," "hearts-a-bustin'," "touch-me-nots," and "grandpa's whiskers" have a charm all their own and a story that's always fun to tell about how they got their names. A gardening friend who is a breeder of iris developed his own 'Graceland' series of Louisiana iris with names like 'Red Velvet Elvis' and 'Lisa Marie Presley'.

Tomatoes are rich in colorful names as well. One of my favorites is 'Radiator Charlie's Mortgage Lifter'. As the story goes, this extra-large, full-flavored tomato was developed by Charlie, a mechanic, who eventually paid off his home mortgage by selling seeds from the giant tomatoes he hybridized in his own garden.

LEFT: *Two boys learn how bold, unpredictable, and wacky gourds can be, as they try to get a grip.* OPPOSITE, ABOVE: *Topiaries—clipping familiar shapes and forms from nature—have entertained us for centuries. As the old saying goes, if you can't beat 'em, join 'em! That's the idea behind inviting these topiary deer into the garden.* OPPOSITE, BELOW: *Touches of whimsy and lightheartedness sprinkled through the garden will always produce a smile. This tiny concrete frog hides in a clump of sweet grass (acorus) near the edge of a garden pool.*

essential ideas

1. Whimsical touches personalize the garden.

2. Humor in the garden adds enjoyment to the outdoor experience.

3. Themes of whimsy running through a garden can add harmony, wit, and surprise.

4. Serendipity can also serve as a form of whimsy.

And what would our gardens be without animals? I can't imagine mine without the pleasure of their companionship. Chickens, rabbits, kid goats, ducks, and, of course, dogs and cats were always a part of my garden as a child, amusing me with their comic diversions.

These days, I have a few chickens. I call my little bantam black Cochins "moving lawn ornaments." Tame and docile and small enough to do little or no harm, they hunt and peck through the flowers and shrubs in search of something to eat, turning up in some of the most unexpected places. The chickens are happy reminiscences from my childhood, and they add another dimension of life to my garden. Beyond their lighthearted charm, they also bring their own benefits to the garden. Bantams eat ticks and other insects, ducks are ravenous consumers of slugs and snails, and, of course, their litter is a source of enrichment for compost.

The houses, pens, and coops for our animals can also add a touch of whimsy, serving both function and fantasy. My honeybees reside in a hive altered to look like an Italian villa—a Bee Palace—fit for a queen and her court. Toad houses, bat boxes, bird feeders, and roosting stations can all provide our gardens with a bit of folly.

Themes are also fun. A single idea running like a thread through the fabric of a garden can add wit and surprise.

A Dutch garden designer I know used the nearby ocean and its many motifs as a theme throughout her garden. At the back of her property, she built a "temple to Poseidon," a garden pavilion erected after a tremendous storm downed one of her large trees. The structure filled the empty spot and provided a place to rest and read. A wave motif made of various stones was applied to paths and paving, and the sound of running water is heard pouring from a shell grotto; everything follows a subtle, yet recurring, water theme. Favorite animals, plants, myths, or ideas can become signature expressions of your own personality and sense of humor.

Sometimes, when elements are presented in the garden in a way that defies logic, they elicit happy surprise. Objects suspended in space or unnaturally supported by water are entertaining puzzlers. This effect brings an enchanted, otherworldly quality to the garden. For a moment, we are spellbound, carried far away to a place where fantasy reigns and wood sprites and gnomes roam and make mischief.

Certain plants, because of nostalgia or their strange appearance, offer their own form of delight. Gourds, pumpkins, Japanese lanterns, elephant ears, and banana trees are jolly in an almost defiant way, flying in the face of modern efficiency and pragmatism. Unlike the more socially respectable petunias and roses, they bring quirky irreverence to the garden.

Something magical happens when we combine ordinary things with a little imagination to create something new and whimsical for the garden. Some of the most satisfying whimsies are temporary, lasting less than a single

season. Scarecrows, twig houses, tepees, and seasonal decorations delight us for the moment; their very impermanence is part of their charm.

The garden is a place that reminds us to not take ourselves so seriously. When you relax and let things happen, all kinds of wonderful surprises develop. Plants reseed themselves and create their own wild garden, a mysterious weed that you didn't pull up grows into a spectacular plant, and Mother Nature plants something for you in a bare spot. As Allan Lacey wrote, "All gardeners need to know when to accept something wonderful and unexpected."

Gardens are also places to laugh. Who hasn't been amused by the antics of birds at a feeder, a hummingbird's acrobatics, or baby squirrels chasing one another? Humorous responses to nature and the garden help us to maintain a healthy perspective and attitude about life.

MASK IN A HEDGE

Add a touch of whimsy to your garden by hanging a mask in a hedge. It is easy to do with a shepherd's hook from a bird feeder and some copper wire.

STEPS
1. Insert a shepherd's hook into the hedge.
2. Anchor it into the ground with a stake and guy wire.
3. Hang a mask on the shepherd's hook.

Mystery

MYSTERY—Piquing a sense of curiosity, excitement, and occasionally apprehension through the garden's design.

It was the darkest dark I have ever seen—an unfathomable void. Large boulders surrounded its entry under the canopy of a virgin hardwood forest. Hickenbotham Cave, a local landmark, had always been a place of mystery and awe to me. Most people approached the cave from the main entrance, but there was a little-known passageway on the backside of my great-grandparents' farm at the end of Dark Hollow Road on the Cumberland Plateau. This enchanted place was my first introduction to the power of a mysterious landscape.

Whenever we visited the farm, the grown-ups would sit on the front porch and spin yarns about the legends of the cave: its lost explorers, Civil War gold, and the cave's namesake, old man Hickenbotham himself. It was said that once, after he had lost his way for an entire day, he emerged from the cave completely white-headed, claiming to have had an encounter with the devil!

All of the imagery and storytelling about this place flickered in my imagination. I can still remember standing at the secret entrance, feeling an overwhelming sense of both fear and desire. In a single moment, I was afraid of the vast unknown before me and at the same time thrilled by the urge to explore what lay beyond. Awe, of course, is a very real response to the wildness of nature, and those same feelings of suspense and wonder should be a part of the garden as well.

Nature herself is full of mystery. The more we learn, the more mysterious she becomes. We are inspired by the design of each secret we uncover in nature, and we can mimic nature's designs in our own gardens. Dark shady corners, vine-covered arbors that offer secluded escapes for flights of fancy, and even quiet retreats from the distractions of everyday life can all provide a sense of mystery.

Creating a sense of mystery in a garden is about using the unknown, the unseen, and the imagination as elements of design. By igniting your visitors' imaginations from the moment they enter your garden, you create a heightened awareness in them. If you design your garden to pique your visitors' interest, they will anticipate that somewhere, lurking in the unknown of the garden, is a surprise—so don't disappoint them.

One simple way to introduce this element is to vary the interplay of dark and light. In other words, plan for shadows—places where both colors and moods deepen, where visitors can escape into soft, dappled shade. A garden without a blend of darkness and light feels stark and soulless. As children we were thrilled to

RIGHT: *A small bridge offers passage over a green-covered pool in the bog garden at Arley, allowing the visitor to pause and ponder what lies below.* OPPOSITE, ABOVE: *A pair of serene and knowing sphinxes were the perfect choice to charge the air with mystery in this cool and quiet woodland garden.* BELOW LEFT: *The forest itself is mysterious to us. This curving woodland path reveals only as much as we are willing to venture—holding the visitor in suspense until it opens in the clearing and the final destination is seen.* BELOW RIGHT: *A passage through a wisteria-covered arch provides a glimpse of a mysterious object beyond drawing us through an enclosed garden full of spring blooms.*

hide in the shade of the shrubs, seeing but not being seen; likewise, as adults, we enjoy the privacy and intimacy of covered arbors and pergolas.

The greatest compliment paid to any garden designer is that the garden is so intriguing that it compels visitors to continue deeper and deeper into its successive rooms; it encourages them to uncover all of its secrets. Simple effects such as moving water—a splashing fountain or a stream trickling from pond to pond—will inspire curiosity and beckon visitors toward its sound. A partially obscured view of a spectacular rambling rose in full bloom can also lure people down a path to get a closer look. A gate, a door, a portal, or an opening that suggests something beyond in a garden will play on our subconscious since we long to see through to the other side. It is always the door that is locked that intrigues us the most.

Paths, and the way we arrange them in our gardens, are one of the best ways to embrace mystery. Once again we see how the element of the unknown is paramount. A curve in a path positioned in a way that it cannot be seen from a certain vantage point in the garden will always encourage the curious visitor to follow its course. Small hillocks and elevation changes in the garden that limit full view of the terminus or destination instill a similar sense of wonder.

essential ideas

1. Mystery in a garden uses the unknown, the unseen, and the imagination as elements of design.

2. Mystery heightens the imagination of visitors, setting up the anticipation of surprise.

3. Intriguing paths tend to invite exploration.

4. Devices in a garden room that play on the senses—sound, sight, smell, or touch—stimulate emotional responses.

ABOVE: *A stone face set in creeping jenny and sedum is a curious feature in a quiet corner of my garden.*

AN INTRIGUING ARCHWAY

Passing from one area into the next through an intriguing arch creates a sense of mystery. You can create a living threshold for your garden rooms with fast-growing plants tethered to a metal arch.

STEPS

1. Plant Leyland cypress to form hedge with a 4-foot gap where you want the arched doorway to go.
2. Have a local welder build the arch.
3. Dig holes for the arch feet.
4. Pour concrete into holes for footings.
5. Place the arch in concrete and allow to set.
6. Tether the tops of the cypress to the metal arch with leather strips.

Sometimes, the mystery takes its cue from the elements themselves. Soil, wind, water, and fire all can have a captivating effect on us. When our hands are in the warm earth, we are somehow comforted. The breeze carries our thoughts to cherished memories and faraway places. Water, too, can have a strangely calming effect on us—the sight, sound, and feel can prompt us to relax and resist urgency. Fire mesmerizes and transfixes our gaze as we stare into the dancing flames.

To know everything or to see everything revealed at once eliminates our opportunity to be delighted by discovery. As Emily Dickinson once said, "The soul should always stand ajar, ready to welcome the ecstatic experience." Tall hedges, hidden bowers, and open gates promise a hidden treasure and encourage exploration. A garden without mystery would be a dull one, indeed. Uncertainty and the unknown make the journey interesting. To follow the winding path, to discover the secret "cave" in your own landscape, and to allow serendipity to appear—all of these should be a part of the gardening experience.

ABOVE: *An open gate accented by lantana 'Miss Huff' stands as an invitation to explore the garden beyond.* RIGHT: *An old iron gate encourages us to make the steep descent through the terraced garden to satisfy our curiosity about what lies beyond.* OPPOSITE, LEFT: *A simple sphere set in a circular basin serves as a contemplative accent in a shady garden. Basic geometric shapes hold their own fascination and mystery.* OPPOSITE, RIGHT: *A bank of overgrown shrubbery has been transformed into a garden feature by cutting out a passage through the center. A small sculpture stands on the other side, luring the visitor into a dark passage and playing on our childlike sense of adventure.*

Time

TIME—Various garden styles reflect certain ages of design.

Oscar Wilde wrote, "Fashion is a form of ugliness so intolerable that we have to alter it every six months." Our insatiable desire for change in the colors and styles of our clothing and home furnishings is an expected, if not greatly anticipated, event in American culture. We have all felt the need to throw out dated clothes or remodel our homes in the latest trends. As we dress, paint, and refurbish our way into this year's styles, we also relegate last year's fashions to a time frozen in the past. The mention of shag carpeting, go-go boots, or polyester leisure suits refers as much to a period of time as it does to a style.

essential ideas

1. Garden styles reflect ages of design.

2. Well-designed gardens have features that are consistent with the age of the house and surroundings.

3. Reproductions of original materials often fail to blend in with the natural aging of the garden.

While we may not be as fickle about plants and garden features as we are about our clothes, cars, and interior styles, similar preferences about what is "in" and "out" have existed throughout history in horticulture and garden design. Formal gardens were all the rage throughout the seventeenth century, a trend replaced by a more natural approach in design by the mid-eighteenth century. Sweeping pastoral landscapes accented with clumps of trees and lakes were transformed from the highly designed and orderly patterns of the former age.

As you design your garden, try to assemble plants and materials that are appropriate to the age of the property or architectural style of your house. Gardens have certain "spirits of the age" that should be met to feel right. Understanding a sense of place is about recognizing its history and connecting the design of your garden with that time.

Plants and materials in your garden rooms can be as incongruous as wearing a tie with sweatpants. A weeping

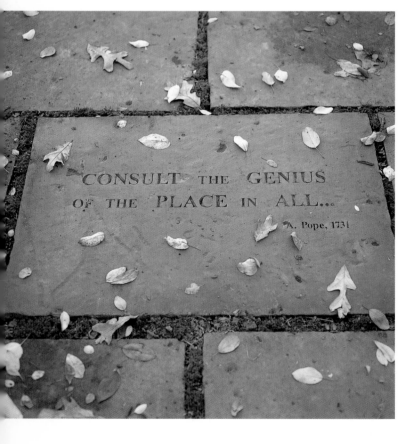

Japanese maple in a New England saltbox cottage garden looks out of place, like a Queen Anne highboy in a craftsman's bungalow. These styles are not synchronized with the time periods we associate with them.

Plants have also served as vehicles of fashion. The latest Johnny-come-lately is always the rage, often pushing out the old standbys, despite their reliability and importance to our gardens. The favorite plants of the previous generation often hold little interest for the current crop of gardeners. Hollyhocks, for example,

LEFT: *These words carved into a stepping-stone just outside my back door serve to remind me that my garden has its own special place in time.* OPPOSITE: *We associate plants blooming with certain times of the year. In the hallway garden on the south side of my house, it's the pearl bush* (Exochorda racemosa) *that trumpets the news that spring is well under way.*

were almost extinct from the American garden scene until a few years ago. Time seemed to have forgotten a plant that was so beloved by our great-grandparents. It was swept away with new attitudes about low-maintenance, evergreen, minimalist approaches to planting—a time when flowers were considered unsophisticated and somewhat a bother. Today, we have come full circle, embracing the "everything old is new again" motto as we celebrate the plants of our past.

Unless materials can comfortably wear the presence of time, they remain foreign objects in the landscape, not really blending in with everything around them. When garden structures and ornaments are made from materials with integrity, they age over time and bear a patina that is honest and real. A garden, by its nature, projects a certain sense of timelessness through its natural cycles of birth and decay. Part of a garden's charm is its ever-changing nature, and objects within the garden need to age with it.

ABOVE LEFT: *The daffodils growing on the hillside reflect the historical time frame of this old farmhouse, lending a sense of timelessness to the arrangement.*
ABOVE RIGHT: *The rustic picket fence that surrounds the farmhouse, true to time and place, further creates a sense of harmony in its agrarian setting.*

RUSTIC TEPEE

Harken back to an earlier time with an old-fashioned twig tepee.

STEPS

1. Select three twigs.
2. Insert the twigs into the ground for support.
3. Tie the top with copper wire.
4. Crisscross smaller twigs up the sides of the tepee, attaching to the legs with copper wire as you go.

Creating Your Garden Home

For many of us, design of any kind is a daunting subject; it frightens us because we are afraid of making a mistake. In Anne Lamott's *Bird by Bird*, the author's brother, who has put off completing a school report on birds until the last minute, is paralyzed by fear as he stares at the blank sheet of paper before him. Feeling frustrated and overwhelmed, he is uncertain how to begin. The solution comes in some simple advice offered by his father. "Bird by bird, Buddy. Just take it bird by bird."

In that same spirit, my twelve principles of design are a "bird-by-bird" method of tackling the project of designing a garden. I arrived at these twelve principles as a result of countless hours walking around gardens, designing gardens for clients, and my studies in garden history. "Framing the View" and "Focal Point" are a product of reading about eighteenth-century landscapes. "Enclosure" and "Entry" arose out of the needs called for in my own garden.

Nature's Role

When I was advising customers at my garden center, they often voiced concern about whether they had the ability to keep their plants alive. I would always try to assure them that although some would live and some would die, it was all a natural part of the gardening process. Over the years, I have killed more plants than I can possibly count, because so much of the work in the garden is about experimentation. This is where planting a garden is different from decorating a home. It would be horrifying if the sofa turned pale, shriveled up, and died, but if an azalea bush gives up the ghost, it can be replaced with something that will thrive.

I used to buy plants from an old nurseryman who had a good sense of humor and a healthy attitude about his plants. The motto for his nursery, written on the entry sign, was "Our plants live, or they die trying." A garden, because of its very nature, never turns out the way you imagine it. Nature is always there, applying the force of change to all your best intentions. So, from the beginning, it's better to get used to the fact that your plans are in her hands.

Many times mistakes can lead gardeners to another level of understanding about the special places they are creating. The "happy accidents" that I have had over the years are nature's way of improving the garden plan. Making a garden in so many ways is like life itself; it's good to have a strategy in mind, but it's a lot more fun if

we can be flexible enough to see the opportunities that lie in the unexpected.

Consider Why

When I am approached by a prospective client, my first question often is "Why are you creating a garden?" If the answer is something like "My daughter is getting married in the spring and we want to have the reception outside," I quickly lose interest. This response misses the point of what gardening is all about. It is a process that requires layering, time, patience, success, and failure, often in equal measure, as well as experimentation and observation. It isn't an object to be purchased and installed in one season to impress friends or provide instant gratification. Instead, it is more like a journey through a series of seasonal experiences—full of challenges and disappointments, but holding great promise. In the end, gardening is an act of optimism.

The twelve principles outlined in the previous section are meant to be a beginner's toolbox, yet they are sound approaches that will grow with you. Depending on the space you are working with, some may be more important to you than others. Above all, you are ultimately the one who makes your garden unique, for a garden cannot help but be influenced by the personality of its creator and steward.

Creating a garden may seem like a matter of extremes, either a blank slate devoid of anything to work with or a mature landscape in need of change. More often than not, the truth falls somewhere in between. Certainly the blank canvas is the most intimidating; with nothing to react to—good or bad—we struggle for a starting point. At least a bad landscape opens our imagination to a better possibility.

When we begin to imagine the garden we want to create, we often go from being intimidated by a blank canvas to letting our fantasies carry us into the stratosphere, envisioning an overly idealized plan that has nothing to do with the reality of our lives. Edith Wharton wrote that the grand houses people build are often based on the fantasy of a party they might have once a year rather than on the actual needs of their daily habits. No garden space can accommodate every whim or notion ever desired. At some point our dreams have to match the reality of the space and the way we live from day to day. A garden that you can enjoy in your regular routine of life is much more important than a space that serves as a romanticized vision.

The Genius of the Place

So how do you, as the great eighteenth-century English poet Alexander Pope said, "consult the genius of the place in all"? And what exactly does a lofty phrase like that mean? Well, for me, "genius of the place" is based on the idea that every outdoor area has the potential to become a garden, but we must first discover how to reveal its finer points and potentialities. Once we understand what is appropriate for a particular garden space, we can reconcile this with what we wish it to become.

To do this, walk around your property and carefully assess the conditions of the site. For every garden, certain circumstances that are influential, undesirable, and unchangeable must be acknowledged and understood. Think about the light, the prevailing winds, the orientation of the house. Does it face the west? Are there elevation changes? How does water drain over the site? What is the soil like?

IDEAS FOR GARDEN
ROOMS

Dining
Entertaining
Barbecuing
Household tasks
Outdoor kitchen
Growing food
Painting
Display collections
Retreat or meditation
Performance stage
Playroom
Parlor
Sleeping
Photography
Utility
Plant nursery
Exercise
Dog washing
Livestock/poultry
Bird-watching
Flower arranging

All of these fixed criteria may seem limiting, but by giving us something very real to respond to, they can stimulate our thinking so that we can make the first important decisions about our gardens. So often we plant a tree because we need shade, then suddenly we see the opportunity in the shelter of the tree.

Engage your senses and listen to your own responses. How does the place make you feel? Is it overexposed with no canopy? Is the light too bright at midday, and is it hot and windy? Is noise a problem? Would you want to linger there, and if not, why?

The next level of becoming familiar with the site involves the release of emotions. What about the site thrills you? If it doesn't excite you in some way, then how could it be improved so that you would feel thrilled? How could it be made more special? Do you long to create a shady nook to slip into and read? How about a place for children to play ball or a rose arbor to walk under as you enter the garden? Would you enjoy getting lost in flower borders full of color and fragrance?

By assessing the conditions, engaging your senses, and releasing your emotions, you connect mind, body, and spirit to the place. This is how you seek out the genius of the site so you can balance the realities of what the area offers with the dreams of what you want it to be.

A fun and engaging way to recognize the potential of your own property is to tour other gardens. Visiting American and English gardens of every size and description was certainly a turning point in my understanding of garden design. As I studied the best gardens and isolated certain features, I acquired a large vocabulary of design ideas and discovered that each plan had the same basic components; the only differences were in scale, climates, personal tastes, and budgets. For a list of national and international gardens you may wish to visit, see page 218.

When you tour gardens, take along the list of the twelve principles and study how each element is reflected in the design. By allowing yourself to respond to a myriad of gardens and see how the principles are combined to convey different atmospheres and moods, you will collect some new ideas for your plan. You will not only train your eye to see these features but also learn how to creatively borrow some of the best for your own garden and adapt them in ways that are appropriate for your site.

Define Your Style

After becoming familiar with your site and visiting other gardens, the next step is to think about your personal style and how to express it in your garden rooms' design. Start by observing how you use your home. Notice which rooms you spend the most time in and what activities you enjoy. If you create outdoor rooms with similar functions, they will become a part of your daily life. Begin the process by creatively thinking of ways to extend your favorite inside pastimes to the outdoors.

Another helpful activity is to gather photographs from magazines, mark images in books, and even select favorite passages from literature to help define your sensibilities. Do you enjoy reading about nature and like to hike and camp? If so, a wild, informal garden may be more to your liking. One of my clients loves textiles and fabrics. Her rooms are a rich mix of tactile sensations—stucco walls, a stone fireplace, chenille throws, and soft, upholstered furniture. For the garden rooms we designed, we chose plants and accessories with the same wonderful blends of patterns and textures.

Another good indicator of your style is how you like to live. If you enjoy having lots of objects around you, that cluttered feeling can be reflected in your garden. Other people are more minimalist in their approach and desire gardens that have clean, edited looks. Instead of a botanical zoo, they prefer closely shorn shrubbery with

EXPRESSING YOUR INTERESTS

LIFESTYLE INTEREST	GARDEN STYLE
Flower arranging	Cutting garden
Cooking/entertaining	Herb garden
Cooking/health	Organic vegetable garden
Travel	Theme garden (Japanese, Italian, French, etc.)
Houseplants	Greenhouse, exotic garden
Woodworking	Bird feeders, furniture, planters, etc.
Painting	Artist garden
Wildlife	Fish pool, bird-watching area, butterfly garden, squirrel-feeding station

crisp, orderly lines. Do you love to travel and cook? A touch of formality along with containers of rosemary, basil, and Roma tomatoes in the garden might reflect your interest in Italian culture and cuisine.

Enjoy the Process

Homeowners do themselves a great disservice if they try to plant and decorate an entire series of garden rooms all at once. The best gardens evolve. However, if time and resources are available, the walls or framework of the rooms can be installed in one season. Then you can take your time to fill and adorn each room, allowing serendipity and your knowledge of gardening to develop. If you rush the process, you will never be able to take advantage of your own evolving taste and style.

"Decorating" the garden home is a different process from decorating the interior of your house. When you purchase a piece of furniture for $2,000, you buy it as is, place it in your home, and except for some wear and tear, it pretty much stays the same. One of the beauties of gardening is that you can buy a $20 tree and with a little time and care it becomes a $2,000 tree. In other words, in a garden, you can grow the look—you don't have to buy the look. How many other purchases actually improve over time, provide daily enjoyment, and increase the value of your property?

Some of my biggest gardening mistakes came when I was in a hurry. I put in my oval lawn before I got the drainage right and finally had to tear it all up, correct the problem, and returf the area. I also chose a fast-growing variety of boxwood to create a parterre and now find myself constantly pruning it to keep it in the right form and shape. A slower-growing, more compact variety would have been a wiser choice. Mistakes happen, but that is part of the grand experiment. Every time I make one of these errors, I take consolation in the fact that correcting problems is all part of the process of working to refine and perfect my original idea.

Do You Need Help?

Garden designers, landscape architects, nursery consultants, and other professionals can offer assistance in many different ways, for varying fees and lengths of time. You can hire a designer to consult with you for just a few hours to help you develop planting ideas for certain areas of your property, or he or she can work with you on an ongoing basis, planning the garden, supervising its construction, and even helping to maintain it over time. Whether or not you need the services of a professional depends on the scale of the project and how comfortable you are with your own skills.

If your plans primarily involve developing a planting scheme, and you are a do-it-yourself kind of person, confident about your talents and style, then following the ideas in this book and striking out on your own is probably right for you. However, if you need guidance, there are several options: You could ask a talented friend or a local garden club member for help; you could take photographs of your property and a plot plan to a nearby garden center with a knowledgeable staff and ask for assistance; or you could hire a professional designer on an hourly basis.

If your plans include "hardscape" projects, such as the construction of walkways, patios, walls, and garden buildings (anything that involves the pouring of cement), you would be better off hiring a professional, unless you are experienced in that kind of construction.

Whether you choose to develop your own plans or work with a professional, the ideas and information in this book will help prepare you to make better decisions. You will be most satisfied with the results when you are an active and knowledgeable participant in the creation of your garden home.

Your Home's Epicenter

Identifying hubs of activity in your home is the next step in creating a garden home. These are the places where you and your family gather and spend most of your time: the kitchen, the den, or perhaps the home office.

Notice how you move through these areas. This pattern establishes the major access of use—how you pour in and out of the rooms. Pay special attention to rooms that lead outside. These outdoor areas should be your first choices for garden rooms. Since the traffic flow in and out of the house is already moving in these locations, adjacent outdoor rooms are the most likely places to be used and enjoyed daily.

These areas also have the best potential for creating both a visual and a functional connection between indoors and out. For instance, a family room might open onto a terrace that connects to a path along a major sight line into the garden, or a kitchen may be connected to a landing or deck that leads to the garage. Continuing the real and visual framework of the house into the garden supports the interconnection between these two realms. Bringing them together visually enlarges both areas and creates a more attractive living space to enjoy.

Throughout history we have looked for ways to create transitions between our shelters and the outdoors, but it has only been during the last fifty years that technology and architectural styles have made this relationship easier to achieve. Homes now feature sliding glass doors, French doors, large Palladian windows, skylights, and lighting; all help to blur the lines between inside and out. *Chimeneas* and other types of readily available outdoor fireplaces encourage us to extend the seasons in the garden.

An excellent transition from one realm into the next is a porch or deck, an area already suspended between inside and out. Porches, patios, terraces, and decks can all serve as preludes into an enclosed garden area or function as garden rooms in their own right.

If there is no direct access outside from your home's epicenter, you can still create compelling views from the windows in that room. Interior windows and doors can be used to embrace views and encourage access to the garden. Here is an opportunity to create a scene that draws the eye outdoors and adds to the feeling that both spaces are connected.

Another place to consider creating a garden room is adjacent to a master bedroom or quiet den. Because these areas don't have busy traffic or a high-use pattern, they offer an opportunity to create outdoor areas with the feel of a peaceful retreat. Master bedrooms in modern homes have become much more than a place to sleep; many have sitting areas that could be easily connected to a garden room. The demeanor and function of these rooms allow you to extend this personal area of your home into a place for reading and relaxing—a smaller and more intimate space with a private deck, a table for morning coffee—separated from the larger, public garden rooms.

Going Outside

Once you have surveyed the interior rooms of your home, studied the views from the windows, and identified prime exterior areas for establishing garden rooms, the next step is to move outside and begin marking the "walls" or boundaries of these spaces, as described in the sections "Enclosure" and "Shape and Form."

You will be tempted at this point to become distracted by several decisions you will eventually need to make. Many people have a long wish list of items they want to include in the design. One wanted to hear the sound of water when she was sitting inside near an open window, so I made provisions for a fountain. Full sun was also important, because she wanted to experiment with roses and sun-loving perennials, so I ruled out shade trees. She also dreamed of developing an attractive garden view from the windows of her house in winter and creating a quiet retreat to spend time in the garden at dusk through the spring, summer, and fall. The clay loam soil in the area was also a factor, as well as hot, dry summers, existing plants, and surrounding buildings.

Even as an experienced designer, I find tackling

SITE MODIFICATIONS

After you look around your property, you may find that the conditions in some areas are not quite what you need.
Here are some ideas on how to transform the site to make it more comfortable and usable.

GOAL	OPTIONS
To warm up an area	· Position garden rooms where they will get maximum exposure from the sun. Southern and western exposures will increase the temperature. · Expose as much of the growing space to the sun as possible. · Add paved areas, which retain heat longer than planted areas. · Create windbreaks with fences and plants. · Use masonry walls for enclosure. · Use hot colors, such as red and orange, in the garden furnishings or the planting scheme. · Use dark colors to retain more radiant heat.
To cool down a garden room	· Prune lower limbs on trees and large shrubs for better air circulation. · Create rooms on the cooler northern and eastern sides of the house. · Use hedges to define the parameters of the rooms. · Plant shade trees and cover arbors with vines as shade from the sun. · Replace paving with more planted space. · Use overhead structures, such as overhangs, awnings, or canopies, to moderate temperatures. They produce shade during the heat of the day while slowing heat loss on a cool evening. · Include a water feature in the space. The sound of water has a cooling effect psychologically. Evaporative cooling from pools and sprinklers can also lower the temperature. · Create a cool and refreshing feel with white and pastel-colored blooms.
To invite the breeze	· Remove lower branches from trees. · Site garden rooms where prevailing winds are encouraged. · Create open-air structures that offer protection from sun and rain but allow the breeze to flow through. · Avoid plantings that will block breezes.
To reduce wind	· Create enclosed outdoor structures. · Plant windbreaks and build fences. · Position living spaces away from prevailing winds.
To make a garden room feel more humid	· Establish plantings that create an overhead canopy that will hold evaporating moisture. · Use low windbreaks that reduce the flow of air. · Replace paved areas with more ground cover or lawn. · Create pools and other water sources. · Use plants and hedges rather than masonry walls for screening.
To make a garden room feel drier	· Create maximum air flow through the space. · Expose as much of the ground to the sun as possible. · Increase the amount of paving surface. · Encourage efficient drainage of area. · Use masonry for enclosure walls. · Use gravel and stone mulches for ground covers.

these challenges all at once to be mind-boggling. My best advice is to focus on the most important things first—the boundaries of the garden room—to avoid confusion and to help you sort through this dizzying array of choices. Forget about the planting requirements, much less the plants. Rest assured that if you get the framework of the garden right from the beginning, the rest will fall into place.

As you envision the outline of the enclosure, keep in mind that you are building a room with walls, doorways, floors, ceiling, and furnishings. The walls will define the room's dimensions and will be punctuated by openings to serve as doorways and windows. The ceiling will also define the space. You may choose to leave it open, or it can be canopied with structures, vines, or trees. The floor of the room can be covered with a variety of mate-

rials from all possible combinations of plants, turf, water, paving, and paths. Finally, the furnishings you choose will decorate the room, making it functional and beautiful. Each element offers an opportunity to express the character and style of a garden room.

Flagging Out the Rooms

Before you begin walking around the site, gather a few simple tools to keep close at hand: a tape measure, a fistful of surveyor's flags, a four-foot rod, and a camera. A sketch pad is also handy for notes and quick drawings. Surveyor's flags are wires topped with brightly colored plastic banners. You can buy them in bundles at home centers and hardware stores; they are indispensable for temporarily marking the boundaries of garden rooms.

First, establish the corners and periphery of the

SITE CHECKLIST

Every site has potential. You will reveal its promise by striking a balance between your ideas for your garden rooms and the site's conditions. Take some time to get to know your property so that you can creatively adjust your plan and at the same time modify the site into a comfortable and appealing space. As you walk around your property, evaluate each area for the following conditions.

CONDITION	CHARACTERISTICS	CONSIDERATIONS
Light	Plants respond best when they are placed in areas that match their optimum light requirements. Consider how the sun may influence the comfort level of outdoor areas. Depending on how you will use the area, you may want to add trees, buildings, or other overhead structures for shade.	• Areas in full sun • Areas in full shade • Number of hours and times of day that receive both
Topography	The shape or lay of the land will influence how it will be used. A west-facing slope will require a different selection of plants than one with northern exposure. A sloping property may call for distinct elevation changes and terracing. Avoid placing structures and garden rooms in areas prone to flooding or areas where the land is not suitable.	• Areas that slope toward the sun • Areas that slope away from the sun • Drainage
Wind	Cold winter winds are often the most damaging to gardens. Windbreaks of trees, shrubs, buildings, or fences can modulate the effect of these strong prevailing winds. They may also provide needed shelter in garden rooms where you plan to dine, cook, relax, or do projects.	• Notice force and direction of winds on a windy day and areas especially affected • Check for areas that are protected from prevailing winds
Soil types	A fundamental understanding of your garden's soil will have a profound impact on your success. Some plants do better in acidic soil, while others require a neutral or alkaline soil. It is also important to know if your soil is sandy, loamy, or heavy clay. If you understand your soil's chemical and physical characteristics, you can select plants that match those conditions, or you can amend the soil to create the optimum situation for the plants you choose.	• Test planting areas for pH • Examine soil for structure—sandy, loamy, or heavy clay • Depth of topsoil vs. subsoil
Water	Water is essential to a garden and should be managed. Too much of it can suffocate the roots of plants and too little will cause stress from dehydration. Some plants do best in wet areas; others thrive in dry conditions. Plant selection should match your site's water conditions.	• Average amount of natural rainfall • Is a sprinkler system necessary? • How is water retained by your soil—does it drain quickly or stand in pools? • How does water drain from your property? • Are there areas of extreme wet or dry?
Noise/ ambient sound	Even the most beautiful garden rooms can be diminished by distracting noise. Consider how ambient sound from traffic, airplanes, and neighbors affects your outdoor areas. While you cannot soundproof your property, you can add elements that reduce the level of noise you experience in the space, such as walls, bushes, or trees.	• Is the noise greater at certain times? • Are there "pockets" that are less affected than others? • Can noise be masked with the sound of trickling water in a fountain, or is there room to build sound buffers?

enclosed areas with one color flag and the paths or other features, such as patios, with another. You can use other delineators, such as bamboo poles, but survey flags are the best. Easy to use and clear against any background, they allow you to see multiple possibilities in a short amount of time. A water hose can also be useful, particularly in laying out curves.

There are no absolute rules for determining the size of an enclosed space, but the most important factor to consider is its intended use. A kitchen garden may need to have enough footage to accommodate raised beds, a potting shed, and perhaps a table and chairs, whereas a small reading nook may require only enough area for a chaise longue and a small end table.

The most pleasing sites are created when the scale of the garden room complements the proportions of the dwelling so that the indoor and outdoor spaces maintain a balanced relationship. As you push the walls of your living space outward, you should maintain the harmony with the interior areas of your home to keep the transition between indoors and out smooth.

Selecting a Shape

Rooms in basic geometric shapes, such as circles, rectangles, squares, or ovals, have a more pleasing appearance. Because these forms tend to blend in with the architecture of the house, they create a cohesive design that connects home and garden. In addition, when the walls of a garden room are living hedges, they will grow and change over time; if you lay them out in a basic shape, they tend to hold their form better.

Remember, the best shape for a garden room is the one that seems to naturally fit the site. What does the area suggest? If you are laying out a room between your home and the sidewalk, a rectangle or square might be the best shape between these parallel lines. However, you may find that an oval or a circle sits comfortably within the four-sided form, with flower-filled corners as accents. Or perhaps you would like to repeat an existing form, such as the curve of a circular drive.

Let the form follow the room's function. The purpose for the room will help you decide how large it should be, and once you flag its size, the shape may be suggested as well. A relaxed room, such as a play area or dining spot, may imply a more informal shape—a circle or an oblong. Another factor to consider is your home's architecture: Is it formal or informal?

As you begin flagging the boundaries of the room, it will be exciting to see the area take shape. To help you get a better feel for its possibilities, use lawn furniture, potted plants, or whatever you have on hand to represent trees, a pool, or other features. Anything that helps you visualize the relationship that each element would bring to the design is suitable. Walk through the space you have marked out and use your emotions and senses to get a feel for how you experience it. Make adjustments to accommodate the changes that best match the mood you are trying to achieve: spacious and open or intimate and personal.

Creating a Series of Rooms

Once you delineate the garden rooms adjacent to the activity areas of your home, the next step is to mark off the boundaries for other rooms with important indoor vistas or places where you would like to create a quiet outdoor retreat near a bedroom, den, or home office. With those boundaries established, begin to work around your entire house, as space allows, marking the boundaries for a series of garden rooms that will completely encircle your home.

As you continue to lay out these connecting rooms, be aware of the adjacent interior spaces to help you determine not only appropriate sizes and shapes but also functions and style. For example, one client needed privacy in her bathroom and dressing area, yet wanted to enjoy the natural light that streamed in only in the morning. The solution was a wall garden outside the windows of the house accented with plants selected to help maintain privacy. A small fountain visible from the bathtub added a soothing touch.

Vary the experience by creating different-sized rooms and keep in mind that one room doesn't necessarily have to lead directly into another. Inside your home, hallways, landings, and small entry areas are important intermediary points between rooms, and they can be useful transitional spaces within your garden as well. Squeezing through a narrow portal and emerging into a larger area can be very intriguing.

Areas that homeowners often overlook are the spaces along the sides of their property. No matter how narrow and dark, they also have potential as garden rooms. Eight feet between buildings may appear impossibly narrow, but it allows enough room for a path and a small planting bed on one side. Learning to maximize the wall space by gardening vertically can yield surprising results.

Even though you may not have the time or resources to develop all of your garden rooms at once, it is a good idea to have an overall plan that you can build on through the years. This way you can be confident that each year's projects will contribute to a plan that will come together over time.

Tackling Large and Small Areas

If you have a large area surrounding your home and you are not sure where to start, the first step is to begin with the space at one side of your house, then divide and conquer. Creating a framework of rooms around your house is a great way to organize your garden. Remember, your home also began as one large space that became rooms separated by walls and partitions. Think of these garden rooms as intentional "additions" to your existing home, new wings that will expand and enhance your living space. By approaching the design one room at a time, your plan will be more reassuringly achievable.

While it may appear easier to create enclosures from large spaces, just as many options are available in a small garden—a fountain can be mounted on a wall; vines and espaliered fruits trees can grow up a trellis or fence. You can garden "on the vertical": There is a world of vines, climbers, and plants ideally suited for tight and narrow spaces. Dwarf and columnar plants are perfect for these areas. With a small café table, chairs, and flower-filled containers, even the tiniest yard can become a garden room. Although it might seem counterintuitive to divide a small space into even smaller ones for fear of making the area too confining, you can create intriguing rooms if you use the right proportions. By screening off parts of the view beyond, you can create the illusion that there is more to see. The key is to make sure you can comfortably use the space, no matter how large or small, narrow or wide.

The Circuit

Once you have determined an overall pattern of rooms around your home, the next step is to determine how you are going to move from one enclosure into the next, creating a circuit or pathway that leads you through each area. This is similar to directing the flow of traffic through the interior of your home.

It is important for the paths to follow your habits when using the space so that the direction they define always feels natural. Ask yourself, "Will I really use this path if I place it here?" If a path takes you markedly out of your way to get from place to place, it will seldom be used. In fact, the most efficient, if not particularly attractive, way to discover where paths should be laid is to note where the lawn is most worn down by walking.

The form or shape of a path in an enclosed space is also important. The best paths are usually simple, direct routes. However, when appropriately sited, gentle curves can add interest, suggesting that something exciting is hidden as you try to see what is just beyond the "bend in the road." Just be sure the paths don't become too complicated, with artificially deep curves. Trying to maneuver along an overly sinuous path takes a visitor's focus away from the garden and can be a frustrating and unpleasant experience.

Four feet is the minimum width of a path for two people to walk side by side and the most common width for a passageway or gate; use a four-foot rod to measure. Another dimension that can be easily measured with the rod is the minimum height of a privacy fence, which is six feet, or one and a half lengths of the rod. Two times the rod's length is the standard ceiling height in many homes, although two and a half to three rods is more gracious.

Laying out the pathway to form an unobstructed line of sight from one room into the next creates a strong axis through the room, which makes the space feel less confining and also directs attention toward an object of interest, as discussed in Principle 3, Framing the View, and Principle 5, Focal Point.

Construct your paths with simple materials. Elaborate motifs in brick or stone detract from the plants. Often the expense of such embellishments is difficult to justify. It is important to use compatible materials that complement your home's style as you build the connection between the garden and the house.

The materials I use for paths in my garden have evolved over the years; I changed materials as I could afford to upgrade them. In the beginning, I used mulch to create paths in the shady areas of my garden and lawn in the sunny spots. As the garden matured and the burden of the initial costs of installation lessened, I replaced these materials with crushed gravel and stepping-stones; for certain paths I used large flagstones.

I see this gradual upgrading as a reflection of my garden's own growth and transformation; it allows me to enjoy the process as well as the results. Changing path materials, adding new plants, and responding to growth and loss through seasonal cycles are some of the most rewarding aspects of my garden.

As you lay out this series of garden spaces by marking off the square footage to accommodate the function of each room and flagging the paths that connect them, you will find that some adjustments are needed because not everything will fit neatly into your design. You cannot shoehorn a four-foot gravel path, a pool, and a planting area into a ten-foot space. Take a deep breath and rank your priorities. Like every other aspect of life, making a garden is an exercise of give-and-take.

One of the best rules of thumb to follow is to clearly define how you want to use each space and stick to it. Trying to assign too many functions to a single enclosure often results in a confused mess. Determine a single primary theme for each area and stay the course.

Framing the View

Whether you are creating a single garden room or a series of interconnected spaces, the next step requires combining two principles—Shape and Form and Framing the View. You will use the shape and form of plants to either screen or frame a view. By blocking unsightly vistas, you create a more pleasing composition within each room, which contributes to the feeling of an enclosed space. At this point do not concern yourself with what kind of plant to use, just stand in the area, look around, and think of the walls as solid masses of varying heights.

The height of the walls can vary, even within the same garden. You need to creatively blend the feel and function of the room with what the site has to offer. Remember that alternating heights can create visual interest and help direct the eye. If you have an attractive view, low walls or hedges will serve as "picture windows" framing the scene beyond. If there is a distracting view, such as a busy street, or if you desire a greater sense of intimacy or mystery in the area, a taller wall is the best choice.

PATH MATERIALS

MATERIAL	USES/CONSIDERATIONS
Grass	Good for broad paths, casual or formal, requires maintenance; not the best choice for heavy traffic areas; low cost to install
Wood chips/mulch	Simple, natural; low initial cost; requires maintenance as chips will decompose over time; good for play surfaces as well as paths; soft, spongy; borders help contain them from spreading, ideal in informal or woodland paths
Gravel	Crisp and clean without being sterile; available in various sizes and colors; durable, long-lasting; tends to be dusty or scatter in high-use areas; blends in formal and informal settings; low cost to install
Concrete (poured)	Low maintenance; remains dry and easy to walk on; can appear sterile; higher initial cost; when cast on site, it can be shaped into almost any size, form, color, and texture; durable; cost effective; requires some expertise to pour and finish
Concrete (pavers)	Long-lasting; wide range of colors, sizes, shapes, and textures to blend with several decors; all the benefits of concrete with do-it-yourself installation; less sterile; low cost
Brick	Versatile; good visual link with brick house and other brick features; can be used in combination with other materials; provides interesting patterns to direct the eye; labor-intensive installation; match durability to use; higher cost for material and installation
Stone (slabs/flagstone)	Natural and enduring; expensive; labor-intensive installation; versatile; effective in both formal and informal garden rooms; wide variety of colors and styles; can provide a connection with house; higher cost for material and installation
Granite, slate, marble	The characteristics of the various stones influence the feel of the garden, from casual elegance to refined, grand or dramatic; higher cost for material and installation; looks best when similar material is used in house; often found in contemporary settings
Cobbles	Rustic and enduring; gives paths a river-washed, aged look; depending on size, they make the path somewhat uneven and challenging to walk on; nice when used as accent areas in patterns; higher cost for material and installation
Tiles	Effective in a variety of applications; numerous colors; sizes, and styles; must be frost-proof in cold areas; can be slippery when wet; better for long, straight paths rather than curves; easy to clean; higher cost for material and installation
Wood	Compatible with wooden fences and trellises; use weather-resistant wood or seals to prevent rot; can be stained various colors; flexible; mid-range cost for material and installation
Mixed mediums	Combining materials can be an effective way to mix higher-cost materials with something more basic and less costly—more impact for less investment

GARDEN ROOM STYLES

FORMAL	INFORMAL
Strong axial relationships between spaces	Organic connections between spaces
Symmetrical composition	Asymmetrical composition
Straight lines	Sinuous, curving lines
Geometric framework	Biomorphic, natural, evolved framework
Plantings with strong, architectural presence	Relaxed, loose plantings
Orderly, clipped hedges	Loose masses of shrubs
Topiary	Natural plant shapes

Another advantage of a tall hedge, fence, or wall is that it serves as a backdrop for plantings. Many plants, such as tall, spiky foxgloves and old-fashioned shrub roses, are at their best when viewed against a solid background that creates a neutral "canvas" on which to "paint" color and texture with accent plants. This high wall of uniform color helps focus the eye on the plants in front of it and eliminates the distractions beyond.

Think of the forms as abstract masses; don't be concerned whether they are shrubs, buildings, or fences. Move these imaginary shapes around to create a composition of forms. Artists employ this process to develop balance and harmony in landscape paintings. At this stage, use a sketch pad to draw the abstract forms as you construct the arrangement. Rough sketches will help you visualize various designs and assess their merits.

Stand in the middle of a flagged room and choose one "wall." Start sketching out forms that would disguise unwanted views and frame the others you want to accent. As you begin to sketch in the large masses and forms to develop the picture, consider how best to arrange the forms so that the scene is visually balanced,

pleasantly arranged, and interesting to look at. As you make these initial decisions and the space becomes better defined, the process gains momentum; it becomes easier to visualize the potential of the garden room.

A sketch pad is also a handy tool for making notes and recording ideas or thoughts that come to you while you are standing at the site. Even the least significant notation can spark a memory or a thought. Later, when you return for a more focused look at the design, notes like "very hot, needs shade," "no breeze," and "canopy would feel good" indicate where you may want to plant a tree or include a place for refuge from the intense sun. They also serve as reminders of the function and style you are trying to develop in each space. These doodles are ways to capture and record ideas, thoughts, and fantasies—expressions that can help you communicate an idea. Many of the advancements in civilization probably owe their genesis to this kind of daydreaming. Your garden deserves no less.

Another helpful tool in this process is a camera. If you are uncertain about trying to record your garden with a pencil, you may prefer to take photographs of each garden room wall from different angles and at different times of the day. Don't worry about how the photographs look so long as they are a good record of existing structures and plants, as well as of the effect of sunlight. To determine scale, ask someone to stand in the space.

Digital cameras let you use your computer to view and print images. If you are developing the prints, order enlargements or make them yourself with a copier. You can then draw your ideas directly onto the copy with a dark marker to help visualize the proposed additions, or you may choose to overlay the photograph with some tracing paper. Outline the "givens" in the photograph, such as the house, trees, or fences, then sketch in the changes you imagine occurring in the space.

A Veil of Privacy

Over the years I have learned that enclosures offer two different levels of privacy—one is real and the other is more of an illusion. Both are important. A real privacy

screen is solid, completely blocking all views into a space: continuous walls, tall hedges, and mass plantings. However, a more open approach with a low wall or fence coupled with a grouping of trees that is not a solid mass gives the illusion of screening and privacy. This approach, where several elements are layered to achieve a sense of screening, is an attractive alternative in certain areas, such as the front of your home.

One appealing combination I have used in my designs includes a low fence, the limbs of a crab apple, and a box-wood hedge. When used along the outside perimeters of garden rooms, the layers allow intriguing glimpses into the area but still provide a veil of privacy. Cascading rose-bushes, tall shrubs, and evergreens also frame views that people walking by can look into your garden through the openings. Like a picture, these views are framed by elements in the landscape to create a more interesting composition than a broad, open expanse of lawn.

Another way to imply, rather than elaborate, a sense of enclosure is with a simple arrangement of columnar elements, such as Italian cypress or other conifers along

a front terrace. The row of trees gives the impression of columns on an imaginary porch. Suddenly the space is transformed into a more inviting, cozy, comfortable place to sit and enjoy the garden beyond. It has become, in effect, a room within a room.

Formal or Informal?

As you combine various shapes to form these masses along the borders of your garden rooms, consider whether you are creating a formal or an informal look. The outline of the room itself suggests a style. You can reinforce that style with the shapes and forms you choose to make up the walls of the garden rooms. Tall

and columnar shapes suggest formality; round, loose forms are typically more informal. (See chart, page 174.)

No matter what style of garden you are developing, there is a combination of shapes and forms that will help to enclose, accent, screen, and frame views. The arrangement of these masses, which will later be translated into hedges, fences, walls, pillars, and trees, is the essence of a well-designed garden, a lasting framework that supports the adornments of flowers and ornaments.

As a simple exercise, arrange three differently shaped objects together on a table. Notice how they relate to one another. Then begin moving the objects into new arrangements. Become aware of how the look

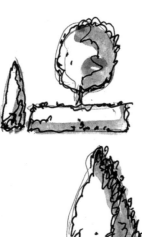

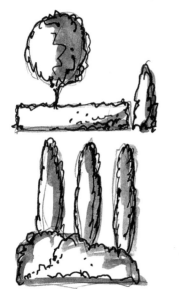

of the composition changes depending on the objects' order and their proximity to one another. As the relationship between the individual objects change, the effect they produce collectively is also changed.

Developing a heightened awareness of your preferences, sense of order, and what you find appealing as you compose the walls of your garden rooms will give you more confidence in your decisions. Understanding the connectedness (or, to the Chinese, the tao), balance (yin and yang), and energy (chi) created by the arrangement of forms are three concepts central to the Chinese philosophy of feng shui.

Choosing the correct height and width for the walls of your garden enclosure is one of your biggest challenges. All too often the proportions are undersized compared with the house and existing plantings. Think about your house and the boundaries of the enclosed space as blocks or abstract forms to help you visualize the best balance for your composition. Walls, hedges, arbors, and trees of the right proportions can help wed the visual mass of your house to the surrounding landscape to better integrate and ground it.

My own one-and-a-half-story frame house is anchored to the garden by a seven-foot hedge that extends out from one side. I see this hedge as an extension of the house, a green "wall" punctuated with an entry arbor and columns that match those on the front porch. The hedge creates a solid backdrop for the flower beds and serves as three walls of my enclosed garden. It had to be tall to match the scale of the house and provide the privacy I wanted for this part of the garden. The result is a space that is truly a room and directly engages the house in a dialogue with the garden.

As you move around your garden room deciding which views to frame and which to disguise or screen, go back inside your house and look through the windows and doorways that have views into those garden rooms. Consider the views from the inside as "pictures" framed by the windows and doors. This perspective may suggest further adjustments to the walls of the enclosures.

Moving from Plans to Reality

Once you are satisfied with the scale and arrangement of the shapes around the perimeter of your garden enclosure, the next step is to choose plants, fences, walls, and structures that replicate these forms. A conical shape drawn on your plan might translate into a spruce, holly, cryptomeria, or pine. Dwarf spirea and conifers can fill in for low, mounded shapes, and rectangles might translate into a hedge, wall, or fence. (Refer to the chart, page 204.)

When considering choices for these forms, you should always search the site for a precedent—something that exists in the landscape that you can draw from and build upon. For example, the fences, arbors, gates, and garden buildings should in some way reflect the look of your house. If stucco is in its architecture, explore using stucco in the walls of the enclosure. Natural and historical precedents are always good guides when creating a garden home that is harmonious with its surroundings. For example, if stone is found locally, consider using it for your walls.

The same holds true for plants: Trees and shrubs that are already growing on your property or in your area are clues to what thrives. Native plants are always excellent choices because they are disease-resistant and require little maintenance. Preserving this relationship between the garden, the dwelling, and the surroundings will strengthen the sense of continuity in a garden home. You strike a balanced and timeless chord between the natural and the man-made.

As you continue to see your garden as rooms with walls, ceilings, and floors, you will understand that the design is as much about architecture as it is about plants. As Vita Sackville-West wrote, "Shape in a garden is so important, if we regard, as I think we should, gardening as an extension of architecture; in other words, the garden as an outdoor extension of the house."

The character of these outdoor spaces, just like that of the rooms in our homes, is reflected in the materials used to construct a garden room's framework. Masonry walls and fences give a more orderly and substantive impression similar to that of dark paneled walls found inside a house. Clipped hedges evoke the same effect. On the other hand, a billowy, untrimmed hedge offers a loose, soft, and less-tailored feel. As you imagine the walls as architectural forms and find the right plants or materials to express those forms, you will achieve the look you want.

To help you sort through all the choices of what to use for the walls of your garden enclosures, consider three things: the conditions you are working with, the style you want to achieve, and your budget. Organize your thinking by dividing the possibilities into two categories: "constructed" and "living." Constructed walls are those made of inert material—all forms of masonry, wooden and metal fences, and so on—while living walls are all the varieties of plants that can be combined to make hedges, screens, or borders.

Constructed Walls

Solid masonry walls always make handsome additions to a garden. They are durable and generally maintenance free. The downside, of course, is that they can be expensive. Masonry is an excellent choice when absolute privacy is required and eliminating noise is a priority.

In cases where masonry would appear heavy, consider the many styles of fences that can complement any home's architecture. A saltbox home, for example, goes well with a picket fence. A wrought-iron fence blends with a brick home and can convey a light and ethereal quality while addressing the practical issues of privacy and security.

It is important to recognize that the more refined the materials, the more formal their application. For instance, marble and granite as building materials are generally used only in the most formal spaces indoors and out. These costly and highly refined types of stone could embellish the gardens surrounding a palace, but would look out of place around a 1900s cottage-style home. The rule to follow is to never use higher-grade or more refined materials in your garden rooms than are found in your house.

If you are thinking of combining materials, such as stone and wood, avoid mixing more than two or three together. For example, if you are building a wall next to a clapboard cottage, a low stone wall topped by a wooden picket fence makes a pleasing combination. In this case, the introduction of another material, such as brick gateposts, could be a distracting contribution unless the brick was carefully integrated into the design of the walls.

When the enclosure extends directly from the house, it is particularly important to select materials that blend with the home's construction, such as brick, wood, or stone, or, if conditions are right, to grow a living wall with shrubs. Creating an enclosure with a hedge is an attractive alternative to fences and walls, but this approach requires special considerations.

Living Walls

To select the best plants for the walls of your enclosure, determine the maximum height and width needed to fill the space and then select shrubs with growth habits that match those dimensions. If you are aware of plants' natu-

ral shapes and mature sizes, you will choose hedges that require only a light trimming to keep them in the desired shape. Hedges with slow to moderate growth are preferred simply because the effort to maintain them is reduced.

You will also have better results if you select plants that are suited to your area's growing conditions and planting zones. Every region has varieties that thrive best in its climate. In the Northeast, yew and hemlock

CONSTRUCTED WALLS

MATERIAL	COMMENTS
Dry stack stone	Rustic, country feel; functional; solid; enduring
Dressed stone	Refined, elegant; range of use from cottage to palace
Brick	Elegant and functional; can be dressed up or down with detailing
Concrete	Simple, modern, functional; can be aged with vines if too stark
Stucco, adobe	Earthy and solid; good background for planting
Wood (panel or boards)	Simple and effective; can be stained or painted to coordinate with house and garden color scheme
Wood (slats)	Casual; allows light and air through while giving a sense of enclosure
Wood (trellis)	Rustic or elegant; support for a living wall of plants
Wood (pickets, wattles)	Rustic or sophisticated, depending on design and level of refinement
Wood (post and rail)	Country/rural feel; defines boundary while allowing views
Wood (wattle twig/bamboo)	Rustic and textured; less enduring
Metal (cast iron)	Elegant and refined; simple to elegant, depending on style
Metal (chain link)	Suburban, affordable, and functional; effective for security; needs a cover of vines or shrubs to fit into garden
Sunken fence (ha-ha)	Pastoral; provides an invisible "fence" to keep animals in or out of an area without impeding the view of the landscape

NAME	ZONE	PLANT PROFILE
Buxus spp. (boxwood)	6–9	Fertile, well-drained soil, prefers partial shade, will tolerate full sun; 3–4' wide x 2–5' tall, depending on variety
Camellia sasanqua	7–8	Moist but well-drained humus-rich acidic (pH 5.5–6.5) soil, 2–3" deep mulch, partial shade (full sun when older); shelter from cold, dry wind and early morning sun, 10' wide x 20' tall
Cephalotaxus spp.	6–9	Fertile, moist but well-drained soil, partial shade or in sun in cool, moist climates; shelter from wind; 10–20' wide x 10–30' tall
Chamaecyparis spp. (false cypress)	3–9	Tolerant of alkaline soils but best grown in moist but well-drained neutral to slightly acidic soil in full sun; 3–15' x 20–130', depending on variety
Choisya ternata (Mexican orange blossom)	8–10	Fertile, well-drained soil, prefers full sun; less hardy species benefit from shelter of a wall; 8' wide x 3–8' tall, depending on variety
Cryptomeria spp.	6–9	Deep, fertile, moist but well-drained humus-rich soil in sheltered site, full sun or partial shade; 3–20' wide x 6–80' tall, depending on variety
Cupressocyparis leylandii (Leyland cypress)	6–9	Any deep, well-drained soil; prefers full sun or partial shade; 15' wide x 120' tall
Cupressus arizonica (Arizona cypress)	7–9	Any well-drained soil in full sun; shelter from cold, dry wind; up to 20' wide x 30–50' tall
Cupressus sempervirens (Italian cypress)	8–10	Any well-drained soil in full sun; shelter from cold, dry wind; from 3–20' wide x 20'–70' tall depending on variety
Elaeagnus × ebbengei cultivars (silverberry)	7–9	Fertile, well-drained soil but will tolerate dry soil and coastal winds, ideally in full sun but will tolerate partial shade; 15' wide x 12' tall
Escallonia spp.	8–9	Fertile, well-drained soil in full sun and shelter from cold, dry wind; 8' wide x 8' tall most varieties
Euonymus japonicus (Japanese spindle tree)	6–9	Well-drained soil in full sun or light shade, sheltered from cold, dry wind; 6' wide x 12' tall
Ilex spp. (holly)	5–9 depending on species	Moist but well-drained, moderately fertile, humus-rich soil in full sun or partial shade; from 10–25' wide x 10–80' tall depending on species and variety
Juniperus selected cultivars (juniper)	2–9 depending on species	Any well-drained soil, including dry, chalky, or sandy soils, preferably in full sun or light shade; a wide range of sizes contingent on species and variety

NAME	ZONE	PLANT PROFILE
Ligustrum spp. (privet)	3–9 depending on species	Well-drained soil in full sun to partial shade; variegated varieties develop better color in full sun; can be invasive; from 4–30′ wide x 5–30′ tall depending on species and variety
Myrica cerifera (wax myrtle)	6–9	Requires rich, moist soil; 15′ wide x 15′ tall
Myrtus communis (myrtle)	8–9	Semi-fertile, moist but well-drained soil; full sun; up to 10′ wide x 10′ tall depending on variety
Osmanthus spp.	6–9 depending on species	Fertile, well-drained neutral to acid soil; prefers full sun or partial shade; shelter from winter sun and wind; up to 30′ wide x 30′ tall depending on species and variety
Photinia spp.	4–10 depending on species	Fertile, moist but well-drained soil; full sun to partial shade; from 15′ wide x 15–20′ tall depending on species and variety
Pittosporum spp.	9–10	Fertile, moist but well-drained soil; full sun to partial shade; variegated and purple leafed varieties develop better color in full sun; from 6–15′ wide x 15–30′ tall depending on variety
Podocarpus spp. (plum yew)	7–10	Fertile, humus-rich, moist but well-drained soil; full sun; shelter from winter winds; from 6–70′ tall and 6–28′ wide depending on species and variety
Prunus caroliniana (cherry laurel)	7–10	Moist, well-drained semi-fertile soil; full sun to partial shade; 15–25′ wide and 20–30′ tall
Prunus laurocerasus (English laurel)	6–9	Moist, well-drained semi-fertile soil; full sun to partial shade; from 5–30′ wide and 3–25′ tall depending on variety
Quercus ilex (holly oak, holm oak)	7–9	Semi-fertile, sharply drained soil; full sun with midday shade; 70′ wide x 80′ tall
Rhamnus alaternus (Italian buckthorn)	7–9	Semi-fertile, well-drained soil; full sun; 12′ wide x 15′ tall
Taxus spp. (yew)	4–8 depending on species	Well-drained, fertile soils; tolerates alkaline and acidic soils; full sun to deep shade; from 5–30′ wide and 18″–70′ tall depending on species and variety
Thuja occidentalis (Eastern arborvitae)	2–7	Deep, moist, well-drained soil; full sun; from 32″–15′ wide and 32″–60′ tall depending on variety
Tsuga canadensis (Canada hemlock)	4–8	Moist but well-drained soil; humus rich, acidic to slightly alkaline soil; full sun to partial shade; from 1–25′ wide and 1–70′ tall depending on variety
Viburnum tinus (*Laurustinus*)	8–10	Semi-fertile, moist but well-drained soil; full sun to partial shade; 10′ wide x 10′ tall.

NAME	ZONE	PLANT PROFILE
Buxus sempervirens 'Suffruticosa' (dwarf English boxwood)	6–8	Fertile, well-drained soil; prefers partial shade but will tolerate full sun if soil is kept consistently moist; 9′ wide x 6′ tall
dwarf azalea	5–9 depending on species and variety	Moist but well-drained soil; humus rich and leafy with a pH of 4.5–5.5; dappled shade; do not plant too deeply as they are surface rooting; a wide range of sizes contingent on species and variety
Ilex crenata 'Dwarf Pagoda' (dwarf Japanese holly)	7–9	Moist but well-drained, semi-fertile, humus-rich soil; full sun to partial shade; full sun for best berry production; 1′ wide x 1′ tall
Ilex vomitoria 'Nana' (dwarf yaupon holly)	8–10	Moist but well-drained, semi-fertile, humus-rich soil; full sun to partial shade; full sun for best berry production; 8′ wide x 5′ tall
Lavandula angustifolia (lavender)	5–8	Semi-fertile, well-drained soil; full sun; 4′ wide x 3′ tall
Myrtus communis 'Compacta' (dwarf myrtle)	8–9	Semi-fertile, moist but well-drained soil; full sun; 5′ wide x 4′ tall
Pittosporum tobira 'Wheeler's Dwarf'	9–10	Fertile, moist but well-drained soil; full sun to partial shade; 2′ wide x 3′ tall
Rosemarinus officinalis (rosemary)	8–10	Well-drained, poor to semi-fertile soil; full sun; 5′ wide x 5′ tall
Santolina spp. (lavender cotton)	6–9	Well-drained, poor to semi-fertile soil; full sun; 3′ wide x 20″ tall
Serissa foetida (serissa)	7–9	Semi-fertile, moist but well-drained soil; full sun; shelter from winter wind; from 12–30″ wide x 12–24″ tall depending on variety
Teucrium fruticans (shrubby germander)	8–9	Well-drained, neutral to alkaline soil; full sun; 12′ wide x 24–39″ tall

are the hedges of choice; buckthorn, elaeagnus, and abelia are found in the West; and in the South, hollies and other broadleaf evergreens predominate. If you are a beginning gardener, you will need to consult your local nursery and gardening catalogs to get an idea of the plants best suited for your area.

Keep in mind that a successful planting is only as strong as the plant's ability to respond to the most challenging set of circumstances. For instance, an inkberry hedge must be planted in full sun with moist, slightly acidic, well-drained soil. If even one of these requirements is not met, the hedge may struggle, and the

When in doubt as to what to use for the walls of your enclosure, go for the simplest solution. When the conditions are right, a straightforward green hedge will almost always harmonize with any style or building medium. It is often easier and less expensive to "grow" a wall rather than build one.

Trees as Hedges

Certain varieties of trees respond well to shearing or interlacing and make interesting "raised screens" for borders. Trees and shrubs trained into the classic "lollipop" form, which is made by carefully manicuring the top into a round ball supported by a single trunk, can be lined up to form a border that creates the effect of a hedge on stilts. In a similar way, espaliered fruit trees trained along a wire act as freestanding screens. These approaches are not meant to serve as solid or opaque screens but are more open, allowing for air circulation and implying a sense of privacy. Knowledgeable gardeners or staff at your local garden center should be able to recommend suitable varieties of trees that can be trained in these ways.

If you are working with an existing landscape, "legging up" trees and shrubs is another way to create a sense of enclosure. The technique involves isolating one or several main trunks by removing other trunks and limbs up to a certain height. This opens the plant in a way that brings in more light and helps to reveal the views beyond.

Legging up is one of the most dramatic ways to give an old garden a face-lift. You get the immediate feeling of greater expansiveness and the space feels less claustrophobic. If a tree or shrub has become overgrown and out of scale yet still holds some merit, consider legging it up and live with it for a season or two before finally deciding on its removal. Often the transformation that occurs with this technique ushers in a new attitude about the plant and the garden itself.

desired effect will not be achieved. So be sure that the total perimeter of the area will provide the right conditions; otherwise, you'll have spots where the hedge will flourish and other areas where it will be weak.

How a hedge is planted and maintained will affect its appearance over time. A common mistake is to space the plants too close together with the thought that more plants will produce a fuller hedge faster. However, what you usually get are weaker plants, particularly if the hedge is to be tightly clipped. Since the plants "knit" from side to side, only the face of the hedge that can capture the sun will be strong and vigorous. Spacing plants farther apart will increase the time it takes for them to grow and fill in, but each plant will be a stronger individual, producing more stems and leaves.

To get the desired look of a wall, it is essential that the plants respond to shearing in a way that makes them dense and solid-looking. My friend Lady Ashbrook refers to this quality as a plant that can take the knife. Knowledgeable staff at a local garden center should be able to help you determine which plants can form suitable hedges.

Another tip to help you keep your hedges looking full is to clip them on a slight bevel so that when they are viewed from the side, the bottom of the hedge is wider that the top. This helps keep the top of the hedge from growing out and shading the bottom limbs from the sun, which makes the lower limbs weak and spindly.

DECIDUOUS SHRUBS

NAME	ZONE	PLANT PROFILE
Abelia × grandifloria (glossy abelia)	6–9	Fertile, well-drained soil; full sun to partial shade; shelter from winter wind; 12′ wide x 10′ tall
Berberis spp. (barberry)	5–9 depending on species	Any well-drained soil; full sun to partial shade; best development of color and fruit in full sun; can be invasive; a wide range of sizes contingent on species and variety
Deutzia spp.	5–8 depending on species	Semi-fertile, not too dry soil; full sun; a wide range of sizes contingent on species and variety
Euonymus alata (burning bush)	4–9	Any well-drained soil; full sun to light shade; 10′ wide x 15–20′ tall
Exochorda racemosa (pearlbush)	5–9	Fertile, consistently moist, well-drained, soil; 10–12′ wide x 10–12′ tall
Forsythia spp.	4–8 depending on species	Semi-fertile, moist but well-drained soil; full sun to dappled shade; from 36″–7′ wide x 1–12′ tall depending on species and variety
Hydrangea spp.	4–10 depending on species	Moist, well-drained, semi-fertile, humus-rich soil; full sun to partial shade; shelter from winter wind; from 3–8′ wide x 2–22′ tall depending on species and variety; climbing hydrangeas can reach up to 50′ in height
Lagerstroemia indica (crape myrtle)	7–9	Semi-fertile, well-drained soil; full sun; from 3–25′ wide x 3–25′ tall depending on variety
Lonicera fragrantissima (winter honeysuckle)	5–8	Any well-drained soil; full sun to partial shade; 10′ wide x 6′ tall
Philadelphus spp. (mock orange)	3–9 depending on species	Semi-fertile, well-drained soil; full sun to partial shade; from 4–12′ wide x 4–20′ tall depending on species and variety
Rosa rugosa (rose)	2–9	Moist, well-drained, semi-rich soil; full sun with plenty of air circulation; 3–8′ wide x 3–8′ tall
Spiraea japonica (spirea)	4–9	Fertile, consistently moist but well-drained soil; a wide range of sizes depending on variety
Syringa (lilac)	3–8 depending on species	Fertile, humus-rich, well-drained neutral to alkaline soil; full sun; a wide range of sizes depending on species and variety
Viburnum spp.	3–9 depending on species	Semi-fertile, moist but well-drained soil; full sun to partial shade; a wide range of sizes depending on species and variety
Vitex agnus-castus (chaste tree)	6–9	Any well-drained soil; full sun; from 6–25′ wide x 6–25′ tall

Designing Entries

The next component to consider when building the framework of your garden rooms is creating a welcoming entry. Pretend there are no house numbers on your street. Without these indicators, how would you describe your house and garden so that guests would know they have come to the right place? What key elements, besides the color of your house, could you tell them to look for that would distinguish your property from all the others? Visual signals that announce the beginning of your garden home's personal space help establish a sense of entry.

The entrance serves as the point of access to your garden enclosure; it offers the first view of the area around your home and sets up anticipation of what is to follow. Like the front door of your home, garden entries become "signatures" of personal style.

As you evaluate your site, ask yourself, "How can I create a welcoming entry?" A common mistake is to make passageways, especially front entrances, too narrow and stingy in size rather than broad and commodious. A comfortable width for a garden entry should be at least four feet wide. As you consider this measurement for your area, take into account the scale of the garden room and house. If the house and garden are large, make the entrance proportional in size; if the dwelling is diminutive, make the entrance smaller.

The landing or stoop at the entry to your residence is another important transition point that should also be considered a part of the garden. A landing mediates between the home's and the garden's architectures to establish common ground. If space allows, make the area large enough to accommodate several people. A good rule of thumb for the size of a landing is one and a half to two times the width of the path as a minimum.

Within the garden, points of entry benefit from the repetition of elements from the home's entry. Specific details, stylistic touches, and materials all serve to knit the house and garden together and provide much needed continuity and a sense of style and order. For ideas and inspiration, browse through books and magazines to find appropriate examples and visit well-designed gardens. Notice how architectural details such as columns, archways, gates, and even distinctly shaped plants can help define a particular look.

Entries can be designed to help you slow down your fast-paced, schedule-driven life long enough to enjoy the experience of entering your garden rooms. Several devices can make the walk seem more relaxed.

Curved paths rather than a more direct approach help to slow the pace and encourage you to remain long enough to "stop and smell the roses." To make paths more interesting, punctuate the walk with clipped shrubs such as boxwood or yew and allow them to bulge into the path to slightly narrow the passageway. Low-growing perennials or ground covers that puddle near the edges of paths soften the lines of a long walkway, giving you pause to stop and look.

Adding steps to areas with slight changes in elevation can also help to extend the experience and give you a sense of "stepping into" a new space. Another way I like to heighten the experience of entry into a garden is through the sense of smell. Aromatic shrubs, perennials, and annuals cause the visitor to slow down and inhale the fragrance of a garden.

The sound of water provides a pleasant distraction and can be even more alluring than the sight. Bubbling water in a wall fountain near an entrance is especially effective when placed in a small area, such as a courtyard, where the enclosed space magnifies the sound.

Plantings along the entrance that invite touch, such as the soft, flannel-like leaves of lamb's ears, are irresistible for anyone passing by. The same holds true for herbs and flowers. The feathery heads of fennel or ornamental grasses nodding into the path reach out to tickle your palms and legs, bidding you to pause along the way. And, of course, we have all been drawn to the beauty of flowers and foliage—their rich and luxurious natures are qualities we enjoy soaking in.

Interior Entries

Creating a strong, clear sense of entry should not be limited to the front of the house or other public points of access to the garden. Each place where a path enters and exits a garden room offers an opportunity to design a prelude to that area. These transitional points define the change from one room to the next and heighten the experience for you and your visitors. When you repeat elements of the entries throughout your garden, they also serve as unifying features that tie the look of the rooms together.

As described in "The Circuit," on pages 171–172, arranging entries through these spaces so that there is a direct line of sight from one doorway to another is a powerful design technique. Being able to see into the next area not only increases the feeling of depth but also alleviates the feeling of confinement. Small spaces seem larger, as if you were looking through a window that is aligned with a doorway inside your home. And when an object is framed within the entrance, this line of sight becomes even more compelling.

Points of Interest

Now that you have the boundaries of your room laid out, with the walls, paths, and entrances in place, the next element of design to consider is focal point. When an object is positioned to draw the eye and create a feature of attention, it becomes a powerful organizing element within the space.

Focal points are important because they give the eye a place to rest and focus. Consider how this works inside your home. If a room is full of colorful and diverse objects, we tend to gaze around until something attracts our attention. When we see something of interest, say a fireplace, we direct our attention toward that object and then begin to absorb the rest of the room. Focal points in a garden enclosure function in the same way by giving the area a visual center.

When using sculpture in the garden, a light hand is the best approach. If brevity is the soul of wit, then simplicity is the soul of design, particularly when placing sculpture or sculptural elements in a space. A single well-sited object of good proportion and composition will serve a garden room better than several unrelated pieces. More than one sculpture clutters the view and tends to be distracting to the eye. Mass-produced forms of sculpture fail to have the same impact as an original design. Once sculpture becomes commonplace, it has a diminished quality, no matter where you place it.

Benches invite you closer, offering a place to stop, rest, and take in the scene around you. Seating should be placed in a garden room to afford the best views while at the same time directing the eye to another focal point or vista. To be effective, seating must be substantial and easily seen, so it needs to have visual weight.

Pots and vases make excellent focal points and integrate beautifully into the garden. Depending on their size and color, they can be as commanding as any piece of sculpture or as subtle as any plant. To create an effective visual statement, make sure the container is ample in size. Scale is a difficult quality to communicate; it's almost an intuitive call, but dare to be bold—bigger is better. In fact, as any interior designer will tell you, oversize pieces can actually make a small and confining space appear larger. You can achieve the same effect by clustering containers together to create a single element with enough impact to make a strong statement.

Siting a garden structure on an important visual axis in the garden can serve as a strong focal point. A toolshed or potting shed designed to reflect the style of your

FOCAL POINTS

ITEM	PURPOSE
Sculpture	Whether abstract or literal, sculpture grabs the eye when it is placed in a garden. Its scale and level of detail invite the viewer to move through the space to draw close enough for a thorough examination.
Seating	By helping to anchor a space, seating invites us to linger and adds a humanizing element to nature.
Containers	Pouring over with annuals or filled with a simple evergreen shrub, containers can be "arranged" just like furniture to help define the space. They are also effective when emphasizing other features such as gates or arbors.
Buildings and architectural features	Utilitarian and decorative garden structures can serve as both eye-catchers and places of refuge. They distinguish the cultivated from the wild.
Windows	Windows offer both light and atmosphere in garden rooms, just as they do in our homes.
Blank wall	A sense of enclosure, mystery, or privacy can be created with a blank wall. Walls can also serve as a backdrop for more decorative elements such as containers, trellises, and climbing vines.
Borrowed views	Objects visible behind the border of a garden can contribute to the garden room by alleviating a sense of claustrophobia within and inviting exploration beyond.
Plants	Either as individuals or in clusters, plants can become visual anchors or serve as living sculptures.
Seasonal shifts	The entire look of a space can be transformed with seasonal plantings of bulbs, annuals, and containers, providing a fresh look for each season. Trees and shrubs have their own "season," too, attracting attention as they bloom or change color.

home and garden can serve both aesthetic and functional needs. Porches, gabled ends, porticos, doors, and other extensions of the house can serve as eye-catchers.

To transform a window on a house into a focal point, simply accent it with a window box below the sill. To enhance it further, add a bench under the window. A pair of containers flanking each side of the bench will complete the composition.

Even a blank wall is an ideal opportunity to create a focus. Use it as a pristine canvas on which to hang objects to draw attention. I've used flower-filled hay baskets, terra-cotta masks, outdoor wall sconces, and even drapery to create effective focal points on walls.

Church steeples or attractive architectural features on nearby buildings also direct attention in the garden. Even a majestic tree next door or a mountain or landscape in the distance can become part of your garden.

A large tree on axis with a prominent window in the house can make a strong beginning for a handsome focal point. The area beneath its canopy becomes a special place to which visitors gravitate. A flowering ornamental tree such as a weeping cherry can punctuate an otherwise uninspired corner of your garden.

Create moving focal points in your garden by emphasizing the changing of the seasons. In late spring, a hedge of blossom-covered roses commands attention; in fall, a fiery display of the maples takes center stage. Each season, plant an exceptional display of eye-catching flowers for borders.

Adding Garden Structures

The final element in building the framework for your garden home is adding structures. Constructed features not only function as focal points but also add utility and style to your garden design.

A list of various garden structures appears on page 99—everything from toolsheds to trellises—but no matter what type of edifice you add to your garden, where you place it is most important.

If the structure is functional and not merely decorative, the first order of business is to make sure that it is located where it is easily accessible. To find the right place, look for spots where it would best integrate into the framework of your garden room. Since space within the enclosure is often limited, the best location for a structure is often within the perimeter, as part of the border. Consider positioning the building along the back wall, with an arbor extending in both directions and tall evergreens planted as a backdrop. This simple composition achieves many goals: It effectively screens one entire side of your property, serves as a point of visual interest, and adds an attractive and comfortable living space, drawing you from the house into the garden.

The raison d'être of a garden is to please, and to be wholly pleasurable, garden rooms must be comfortable. Structures provide us with a sense of place that encourages us to visit and linger. They offer shelter from the wind, rain, and sun, yet invite us to be outside. A garden building positioned within a garden room thus becomes a room within a room.

Designing or remodeling garden buildings offers you another opportunity to create continuity and harmony between your house and your garden. As you peruse magazines and books and study other gardens, notice how the roofline of a structure is its most defining feature; scale and proportion are critical, too.

I once remodeled a 1940s utility building into a small cabana. Luckily, the owner discovered enough

matching glazed terra-cotta tile stored under the house to complete the roof. The pitch of the roof emulated that of the house, and the tile matched perfectly. To further harmonize this scheme, we painted the cabana a dull gray green, the same color as the house. By attending to these few crucial details, we transformed a boxlike structure into an elegant place for leisure.

To make the most positive impact, buildings should appear substantial and reflect permanence and sustainability. A strong and bold presence in the landscape is reassuring and comforts us on a subconscious level.

One of my clients asked me to integrate a deck that was suspended from an upper story into the garden below. The tall posts that supported it gave it a gangly, unfinished appearance. As the backyard was rarely used and seen only from the vantage of the deck, its underpinning had never been a priority. However, from below, the view of the underside of the deck dominated the entire space. It ran the entire width of the house and stood a full story high, overwhelming both the house and the garden with its dark, looming presence.

The solution was to anchor the deck to the ground visually and connect it to the garden. We paved the floor under the deck, covered the sides with a diagonal lattice grid, and punctuated the center with a gate that opened out onto the lawn. These lattice walls could then serve as a trellis for growing roses and enclose the space under the deck, creating a structure to store garden tools and supplies.

Enhancing this single element metamorphosed the space. As a result, one entire plane or wall of the garden was defined, and the deck had a proper base that made it appear secure and substantial. The framework was successful in part because the proportions of the underpinning were harmonious with the scale of the deck. Conventional prefabricated lattice panels would have been undersized and too refined. The diagonal arrangement of the one-by-four-inch lumber gave it the visual

weight it needed to support the deck above and transform its spindly, precarious character.

Look around your property and see what you have available to build upon. One of my garden designs presented the challenge of transforming an old metal storage unit into an attractive and desirable feature in a small garden. It was a small eight-by-ten-foot structure with a low pediment on the front that had no character, good or bad, to speak of. After painting it a dark color, I applied a lattice motif to the sides and attached wooden pilasters to make a more classical pediment. These decorative changes, coupled with a climbing rose that covered the top, transformed a building of utility into a fun and whimsical garden feature.

If your budget does not allow for cosmetic surgery, you may need to resort to methods of concealment. Sometimes it is best to simply screen or hide buildings that add nothing to the design of the garden. As Frank Lloyd Wright once said, "The physician can bury his mistakes, but the architect can only advise his client to plant vines." Clinging vines and well-placed shrubs can diminish the impact of an unattractive structure while providing a wall of green that can reinforce the architecture of the garden home itself.

Garden buildings are also opportunities to have some fun and reflect your own personality and personal style. A garden "folly" is a whimsical structure for fun and entertainment that was a popular eighteenth-century English idea. Modern garden follies have taken the form of cabanas, gazebos, and belvederes. You have an opportunity to merge the functional with the delightful by transforming ordinary buildings of utility, such as potting sheds and storage buildings, into fun-loving, attractive garden features.

Attached Rooms

Porches, decks, verandas, loggias, terraces, and patios are the most obvious and direct extensions of the house. When covered by roofs, they protect us from the elements and become transitional areas between inside and out. In open-sky rooms, the floor and walls become the defining elements, imparting size and style to the room.

Porches evoke a certain warmth and nostalgia in us. I have fond memories of Grandmother Smith's farmhouse and her array of entry plants that spilled down the steps of the porch. Her favorite houseplants were displayed in every container imaginable—coffee cans, old tureens, and even a few white enameled pots and discarded kettles. Reflecting years of care and admiration, they started out as slips and cuttings given to her by friends and family. This simple and honest entrance, lovingly composed and unaffected, made a lasting impression on me.

A loggia is an outdoor living space incorporated into the plan of a house. It is like a porch but is bordered on several sides by the walls of the other rooms of the house. It provides the comfort and security of an interior room yet allows you to enjoy the sights, smells, and sounds of the outdoors. It, too, creates a connection between inside and out.

My loggia is a covered extension between the house and the garage. The open sides permit unobstructed views from one side of the garden to the other. Like my indoor dining room, my loggia serves mainly as an eating area, but it also functions as a place where I write, work on my beehives, arrange flowers, and paint. Some of my most memorable dinner parties have been relaxed gatherings of friends dining alfresco on the loggia. When the garden is aglow with torchlight, and a nocturnal chorus of crickets and cicadas serenades us, the loggia is magically transformed into a beautiful, romantic setting.

Overhead Structures and Supports

Whether you call them arbors, pergolas, awnings, or bowers, overhead structures serve as "ceilings" to garden rooms that merge garden and sky. They can be free-standing or attached to a building. These sheltering enclaves not only create a greater sense of intimacy and privacy but also protect us from the elements.

Arbors serve many roles in the design of a garden. There is just something more satisfying and pleasing about walking along an arbor-covered path instead of the very same path without its leafy canopy. Perhaps we are drawn to its sense of protection and shelter, or maybe the play of light and shadows makes it more interesting and appealing to the eye.

Whether rustic or refined, arbors add a romantic and mysterious quality to a garden room. You can cover them with a wide range of plants—just try to match the plant with the style of the structure. For instance, more rustic or vernacular arbors that recall the farm gardens of yesteryear suggest vines associated with country life. Wild grapes or muscadines and other native plants, such as trumpet vine, woodbine, and Virginia creeper, are ideal. Gourds and morning glories are fast-growing and exuberant additions to an arbor. A more refined arbor calls for elegant apparel. The genteel qualities of roses, clematis, and jasmine are better suited to this style and offer the added dimension of their sweet perfume from the scented flowers growing above.

These structures need not always be covered with plants, but the foliage helps to soften the overall presentation and enhances the transition into the garden. While wisteria, clematis, and trumpet creeper are some of the fastest-growing vines for covering these types of structures, climbing roses also hold popular appeal.

I once covered a long rustic arbor made of rough cedar poles with the rose 'Mermaid'. If you are not familiar with this rose, beware, because it has its own special lease on life. In just three short seasons this rose almost covered the entire thirty-foot length of the arbor, and just before the yellow flowers opened, the golden buds made it appear as though the entire arbor were enshrouded in a canopy of goldfinches.

One of the most ancient garden structures is the bower. Originally designed as a small shelter for farmers and shepherds, the bower evolved into a decorative garden structure that still offers protection from the elements and a place to rest. In its simplest form, its roof is made from entwined boughs of trees or shrubs. Bowers can also be constructed from wood and covered in lattice. I have created bowers by hollowing out an appropriate amount of space for a garden seat from a mass of shrubs. Rampant growers such as elaeagnus and for-

sythia are ideally suited to clipping out an arched alcove to make a quiet place to rest or read.

Plant supports are also considered a form of garden structure that can contribute to the style of your garden room. Depending on the look you are developing, these structures can be as simple as twigs to make hoop rings for your sugar peas in the vegetable garden or bamboo and twine tuteurs. These seasonal supports are movable, changeable accessories. More permanent structures for supporting plants are obelisks, tuteurs, fences, and trelliage made from wood or metal. Just the slightest suggestion of underlying bits of architecture adds so much to the garden's composition. Support structures can also be used to help vines onto buildings. This serves to soften the building's sharp edges further integrating the structure with the garden. A rose along the edge of a roofline or a wisteria growing horizontally across the facade of a house can go a long way toward bringing the garden and architecture together.

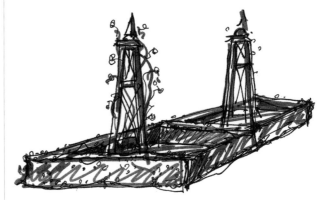

The Garden's Soul

If we look at the garden as a body, the hedges, fences, paths, and other structural features serve as its skeletal framework, or bones, giving the body size and definition, and the flowers, furnishings, and other elements of decor constitute the garden's soul, giving the body its spirit, nature, and personality. Striking a harmonious balance between the body and the soul creates a beautiful and whole being.

Now that you have the body or framework of your garden home in mind, you can use the principles of Color along with Texture, Pattern, and Rhythm, Abundance, Whimsy, Mystery, and Time to help you develop the soul of your garden rooms.

You will find that the first six principles work together to create a whole, while these last six function more independently. Each element has its own personality and can be applied in varied measure depending on your own individual style. Color may come to dominate one garden room, with the other five elements playing a supporting role. Or perhaps you prefer to let pattern, texture, and rhythm guide the design, opting for fuzzy and variegated plants with not much variation of color.

As your garden style evolves over time you can create different moods in each room by simply changing the degree to which each principle is present in the composition. Much like repainting your living room walls from white to red, or switching the slipcovers on the sofa from a aggressive pattern to a neutral solid, bringing one of these elements of embellishment to the forefront of your garden's design changes the overall feel and points of interest. With that said, it is also important to remember that while one of these elements can have a starring role, it is the supporting cast, working together, that completes each scene of your garden rooms.

Essential Ideas of Color

Color adds mood, energy, and character to your garden. As you think about what color scheme you would like to use for each room, you may find it helpful to review "Essential Ideas" on page 108.

The color wheel is also a useful tool to help organize the hues of the spectrum and understand their relationship to one another. Colors that are adjacent or close to one another on the wheel, such as yellow and orange, are considered harmonious or analogous colors. Colors

that are directly opposite one another, such as red and green, are considered complementary colors. These contrasting combinations can produce the most striking and vibrant distinctions. Combinations of opposites, such as orange and purple or yellow and blue, will "pop" in your garden rooms just as they do inside your home and create a jolt for the eye. Reading about the maxims of color theory is one thing, but putting them to work in your garden is quite another matter. To help you through the color maze, here are some of the basic color choices in the garden with ideas on how to use them effectively in various combinations.

GREEN. Understanding how to use green creatively with other colors is one of the keys to creating a memorable color scheme. Green is the foundation color of most gardens. If the living framework of your garden room is shrubs and trees, it is swathed in various shades of green. All other colors are laid upon this congenial tapestry.

Green is also a color that constantly changes through the seasons. In spring, greens are accented with fresh, clear, vibrant shades. By summer, greens deepen and become a backdrop to the season's ephemeral flowers. As other colors fade in winter, the somber-colored evergreens remain, offering the promise of spring's renewal. The shifting shades of the green framework seem to naturally coordinate with the predominant flowers of each season.

WHITE. White flowers tend to glow in the garden as evening falls, flickering like radiant candles in the fading light. 'Madame Plantier', 'Katharine Ziemet', and 'White Pet' are just a few of the white roses that shine at twilight, appearing to almost emit a soft luminosity stored during the day. Later in the summer, after the roses have made their initial splash, the sparkle is maintained with 'Regale' lilies, white phlox 'Admiral', nicotiana, and white balloon flowers.

An all-white garden evokes a restful, calm feeling, particularly when there is a range of various hues of greens on hand to lend support to the composition.

Silvery grays and glaucous foliage help to segue sparkling whites into darker shades of green. Without this transition of "support greens," the contrast might seem too abrupt. Variegated foliage marbled with a range of pale greens to creamy whites can also help soften these transitions. The foliage of plants like *Liriope* 'Silver Dragon' and variegated winter creeper can lighten a dark corner and offer a bridge for white flowers to the darker greens.

GRAY. As the consummate diplomat in the family of colors, gray mediates among various personalities of the color wheel. I use it between color extremes, such as the raging brilliance of orange or red and the soft whispers of pastels to bring balance and concord. The gray-green foliage of artemisia, lamb's ear, Scotch thistle (*Onopordum*), and elaeagnus effects harmony because gray is all of the colors combined. I made this discovery not in the garden but standing in front of my easel.

I was plein-air painting with some artist friends in a beautiful outdoor setting along the California coast. After the session, we were cleaning off our palettes when one of the artists scraped all of her remaining oil paints together, mixing the myriad of hues into a single gray-green color that is reminiscent of gray foliage plants like lamb's ear. She saved this as a base coat for many of her large paintings. All the colors on her palette, combined with white, blended into the color gray — no wonder it feels so right in any color scheme. The neutrality of gray makes it a perfect mixer that crosses all color boundaries and brings a level of calm to virtually any situation. When in doubt about what color to add, gray-greens are often a safe bet.

BLUE. Blue is easy on the eyes and feels carefree. It is almost impossible to get too much blue in a garden. It seems to cast an almost magical spell wherever it appears. Blue flowers, and to a lesser degree pastels, can give a garden a greater sense of expansiveness. Because blue is the color that meets the horizon and the sky beyond, it supports the illusion of greater distance. That's why porch ceilings are often painted "bird's-egg blue." Insects think a ceiling painted blue is the sky and are less prone to land on it. Even nature can be fooled by this illusion.

There seems to be a blue for every color scheme, and certain color combinations enhance its qualities. Try mixing pale buttery yellows and cream-colored flowers with blue. Blue in all of its forms is a natural with gray plants and glaucous foliage. Sea hollies (*Eryngium* species), balloon flowers, and *Salvia* 'Indigo Spires' seem more brilliant when set against silvery gray artemisia and lamb's ears.

Blue is always refreshing in the garden, but it is particularly striking in early spring. Blue pansies and grape hyacinths are a favorite in combination with pale yellow miniature daffodils such as 'Hawera' and early pale pink tulips. Later in spring, the Spanish bluebells, blue columbine, lady bells, and spiderworts all lend their own touch of blue to the shade garden.

Among the blue flowers, the coveted and difficult to grow Himalayan blue poppy (*Meconopsis grandis*) is touted as the bluest of them all. When I first saw this flower, I realized that others I had been loosely calling blue were actually blues with varying amounts of red in them,

FAVORITE COLOR COMBINATIONS

1. Salmon to peach combined with:
   Chartreuse
   Gray
   Blue
   Cream

2. Magenta/pink combined with:
   Burgundy
   Lavender
   Gray
   Cream

3. Clear to pastel yellow combined with:
   Blue
   White
   Variegated foliage

4. Orange combined with:
   Purple
   Hot to medium pink
   Chartreuse

5. Scarlet red combined with:
   Orange
   Purple
   Golden yellow

GHOSTLY GRAYS—TO HARMONIZE

Artemisia 'Silver Queen' (wormwood)

Cerastium tomentosum (snow in summer)

Eryngium giganteum 'Silver Ghost' (sea holly)

Helichrysum petiolare (licorice plant)

Onopordum acanthium (Scotch thistle)

Perovskia atriplicifolia (Russian sage)

Salvia argentus (silver sage)

Santolina (lavender cotton)

Senecio cineraria (dusty miller)

Stachys byzantina (lamb's ears)

Verbascum 'Arctic Summer' (wooly mullien)

WHITE/VARIEGATED—TO SPARKLE

Aegopodium podagraria 'Varigatum' (bishop's weed)

Armoracia rusticana 'Varigata' (variegated horseradish)

Arum italicum

Brunnera macrophylla 'Variegata' (variegated Siberian bugloss)

Cornus alba 'Elegantissima' (variegated red-twigged dogwood)

Euonymus fortunei 'Silver Queen' (variegated winter creeper)

Hedera algeriensis 'Glorie de Marengo' (variegated Algerian ivy)

Hedera helix 'Anne Marie' (variegated English ivy)

Hosta—numerous cultivars with white leaf margins and variegation (plantain lily)

Hydrangea macrophylla 'Mariessii Variegata'

Ilex aquifolium 'Silver Milkmaid' (variegated English holly)

Iris pallida 'Variegata' (variegated iris)

Lamium galeobdolon 'Variegatum' (yellow archangel)

Liriope 'Silver Dragon' (lily turf)

Lunaria annua 'Variegated'

Mentha suaveolens 'Variegata' (pineapple mint)

Miscanthus sinensis 'Variegatus' (eulalia grass)

Phalaris variegata (ribbon grass)

Polygonatum odoratum 'Variegatum' (variegated Solomon's seal)

Sedum 'Frosty Morn' (stonecrop)

Thymus vulgaris 'Silver Poise' (silver thyme)

BURGUNDY/DARK RED —TO DEEPEN

Ajuga reptans 'Burgundy Glow' (carpet bugle)

Berberis thunberggi (red barberry)

Beta vulgaris (ruby chard)

Canna 'Black Knight' (Indian shot)

Cercis canadensis 'Forest Pansy' (red bud)

Colocasia (taro)

Cotinus coggygria 'Royal Purple' (smoke tree)

Foeniculum vulgare 'Purpureum' (bronze fennel)

Heuchera 'Palace Purple' (coral bell)

Ipomoea 'Blackie' (sweet potato)

Lysimachia ciliata 'Firecracker' (loosestrife)

Ocimum basilicum 'Dark Opal' (purple basil)

Penstemon digitalis 'Husker's Red'

Prunus cerasifera (purple leaf plum)

Red cabbage

Sedum maximum 'Atropurpureum' (stonecrop)

Solenostemon—numerous cultivars (coleus)

Weigela florida 'Foliis purpureis'

CHARTREUSE—TO ELECTRIFY

Acorus gramineus 'Ogon'
(golden variegated sweetflag)

Alchemilla mollis (lady's mantle)

Berberis thunbergii 'Aurea' (golden barberry)

Buxus sempervirens 'Marginata'
(golden boxwood)

Carex 'Ever Gold' (sedge)

Caryopteris 'Worcester Gold' (bluebeard)

Chamaecyparis—many golden cultivars
(false cypress)

Coleus 'Gold Wizard'

Eucomis bicolor (pineapple lily)

Euonymus fortunei 'Emerald and Gold'
(variegated winter creeper)

Euphorbia amygdaloides 'Robbiae'

Helichrysum petiolare 'Limelight'
(licorice plant)

Hosta—numerous golden and chartreuse
cultivars (plantain lily)

Humulus lupulus 'Aureus' (golden hops)

Ipomoea 'Margaretia' (sweet potato)

Lysimachia nummularia 'Auralia'
(golden creeping Jenny)

Melissa officinalis 'Aurea' or 'All Gold'
(lemon balm)

Philadelphus coronaria 'Aureus'
(golden mockorange)

Spiraea japonica 'Gold Mound'

Taxus baccata 'Aurea' (golden yew)

Thymus × citriodorus 'Aureus'
(lemon thyme)

Yucca 'Golden Garland'
(Spanish bayonet)

GLAUCOUS/GRAY-GREEN—FOR TRANSITION

Agave americana (century plant)

Anaphalis triplineruis (pearly everlasting)

Artemisia—many species and cultivars

Athyrium niponicum 'Pictum'
(Japanese painted fern)

Broccoli

Buddleia davidii (butterfly bush)

Cerinthe major 'Purpurascens'

Cynara cardunculus (cardoon)

Dianthus gratianopolitanus 'Bath's Pink'
(pinks)

Elaeagnus × ebbengei cultivars
(silverberry)

Eryngium yuccafolium (rattlesnake master)

Eucalyptus (gum tree)

Fescuta glauca (sea urchin fescue)

Gypsophilia (baby's breath)

Hosta—many glaucous-green cultivars

Lamium 'White Nancy' (deadnettle)

Lavandula (lavender)

Macleaya cordata (plume poppy)

Melianthus major (honey bush)

Plectranthus argentatus

Romneya coulteri (Matilija poppy)

Rosa glauca (rose)

Ruta graveolens (common rue)

Salvia officinalis (cooking sage)

Sedum reflexum (blue spruce stonecrop)

Sedum spectabile 'Autumn Joy'
(stonecrop)

Sedum spurium 'Vera Jamison'
(stonecrop)

Yucca filamentosa (Adam's needle)

which made them more violet than blue. I began to look more closely at colors and to appreciate their subtleties.

YELLOW. There are legions of early-blooming yellow flowers that break through winter's darkest days. Bright, perky, almost puckish, yellow is the color of the growing season's first flowers—daffodils, crocus, forsythia, corylopsis, and mahonia. These bright, cheerful yellows warm the barren winter landscape. But as summer approaches, you can turn down the heat of these vivid yellows by embracing soft, yellow pastels such as yarrows, Coreopsis 'Moonbeam', and buttery daylilies. When summer gives way to autumn, return to the rich golden yellows of goldenrod, dahlias, chrysanthemums, and helianthus.

Yellow is effective in measured amounts, like the sun. Too much seems to overwhelm an area, so use it sparingly. It sparkles in combination with purple, lavender, and blue. Clear, acid yellows look fresh and clear when blended with cream and ivory flowers. One of my favorite daylilies is an old variety called 'Hyperion'. It is a bright clear yellow. I grow it for its tall elegant scapes and slightly fragrant flowers. However, 'Hyperion' is a very bright in-your-face yellow, so I have worked at toning it down just a bit by creating some hybrids that are more pastel yellow but retain the height and scent of 'Hyperion'.

Use a light hand with yellow or yellow-green foliage plants as well. The intensity is too rich if too many are planted in a single area. The plants will look sickly and unnatural, just the opposite of bright accents in the garden. In dark, shady areas of your garden, golden-hued foliage offers a warm glow—as though a ray of sunshine had found its way through the canopy of trees to illuminate a favored plant.

RED. Red is a color that demands immediate visual attention. Unlike diffuse blue, red jumps forward as a salient reminder of its dominance. If you look at a painting or a room decorated with a touch of red, your eye will focus on the color immediately. The object will seem closer to you than it really is. This illusion can have practical applications in the garden.

If you want a small space to feel larger and seem more expansive, use blues and pale lavenders; reds warm up and enclose a room. Large areas of reds, particularly those mixed with yellows, can be somewhat jarring, especially in a small area.

Bold, confident, and self-assured, reds should be used sparingly. From the orange-reds made warm by the addition of yellow to the blue-reds in magenta and crimson, all reds strike a commanding pose in the garden.

Recognizing the duality of reds was one of the first lessons I learned when I began creating color combinations. I was innately drawn to what felt like the cooler side of red. Roses such as 'Russell's Cottage' (Rosa russelliana) and 'Veilchenblau' attracted me because of the depth of their blue-red, almost violet hues. When paired with a range of clear vibrant pinks to soft, chalky pastels, this family of reds spans the entire spectrum of cool reds. Mixing cool and hot reds together has always been tricky. Bringing the two families together in a composition is reserved for the most fearless of gardeners. When warm and cool reds collide, the visual effect is quarrelsome and dissonant. Embrace one family or the other and build on its strengths.

You can plan your garden so that the "temperatures" of red follow the seasons. Use cool reds and pinks in early summer when the days are shorter, cool, and crisp. As the season warms, let the warmer reds come into bloom. By late summer, the orange reds will begin to feel more suitable. Use sizzling red as the season drifts toward fall, when your hot-colored flowers will ultimately be met by a blaze of autumnal foliage.

Roses can be a wonderful source of the entire spectrum of reds and pinks in the garden. The blooms of old-fashioned shrub roses range from deep cerise to almost white, except for the slightest blush of pink. These colors can be supported by the burgundy-claret-colored foliage of the purple smoke tree (*Cotinus* species), barberry, and *Heuchera* 'Palace Purple', which adds a richness and depth to the overall composition. These deeper colors help to anchor the lighter, more ethereal tints of the same color family. The softest of these pinks can be seen in the roses 'New Dawn' and 'Blush Noisette'. Deeper hues are paled with varying amounts of white, producing a gradient of pinks and mauves. If the flame of red burns too bright, you can tone it down by associating it with its complement. Hot, fiery reds planted with saturated purples such as *Salvia* 'Indigo Spires' or *Salvia guaranitica* can help ground an intense red color. The cooler purples allow the eye to mediate the warmth of the reds to make them feel less abrupt and garish. Foliage, too, can subdue red. Foliage tones are rarely as pure and bright as the colors of flowers. The smoky maroon leaves of *Canna* 'Black Knight' and the mahogany red of *Dahlia* 'Bishop of Langdaff' or 'Thomas Edison' offset the intensity of *Crocosmia* 'Lucifer'. These dull reds make the intense members of the family more palatable and easier to live with.

ORANGE. So many of the names we use when describing orange and its rich diversity are drawn directly from the garden and nature—peach, persimmon, pumpkin, bittersweet, salmon, and coral. All are helpful in discerning the subtleties of this warm and friendly family.

PURPLE. Purple is the complement to orange on the color wheel, so when they are paired, the contrast is intense and vibrant. Purple in all its shades and hues is a wonderful color to use in the garden. The soft whisper of pale lavender in the form of Russian sage and asters brings a transcendent quality to a flower bed. When pink and blue-violet are merged, purple becomes mauve, a color that can help connect lavender and paler shades of violet to richer shades of crimson, plum, and claret. In its darker tones purple feels luxurious and royal, adding depth and providing visual weight to ethereal colors. By late summer, when the salvias are at their best, purple is present in all its forms. Asters, maroon dahlias, the pods of hyacinth beans, hardy ageratum, and the dark plumes of *Buddleia* 'Black Knight' make this time of year rich in purple.

Your Color Style

Color is an effective tool in reflecting your personal style. Look inside your home to find which colors you seem to favor. Coordinate color combinations outside just as you would indoors. When interior rooms look out onto garden areas, you can blend the rooms together by extending the same color scheme into those exterior spaces. Colors of awnings, seat covers, and patio furniture can also take their cue from adjoining interior areas.

Another place to check for your favorite colors is your closet. Do certain colors make you feel bright and happy when you wear them? What colors put you in a romantic and relaxed frame of mind? Think about extending those color "moods" into the atmosphere of your garden rooms.

When you select color schemes for garden rooms, you also need to consider your home's exterior color, especially in outdoor areas that adjoin your home. As you move away from the house, and it is not as dominant in the view, its color diminishes in importance. You can then gradually shift the colors in your garden away from those that are the most compatible with the house to create subtle variety.

If you are still baffled about selecting colors for your garden rooms, consider the opening stanza of the poet William Blake's lyric "Auguries of Innocence":

To see a World in a Grain of Sand
And a Heaven in a Wild Flower,
Hold Infinity in the palm of your hand
And Eternity in an hour.

What better source for inspiration than nature herself? Single flowers can be wonderful guides to eye-catching color blends. If you look closely, you will discover that every flower is made of many colors, and these arrangements of hues are effective teaching tools when using color on the larger canvas of your garden. This technique is especially helpful when I am challenged to use a color that is not one of my favorites, such as orange.

The popular lantana cultivar 'Confetti' is a study in color you can capture in a single glance. Deep orange, salmon, pink, yellow, and cream can all be found in the tiny florets of each bloom. Here orange is not boisterous and brash but adds depth and weight to the color scheme. Another surprising color combination is found in purple coneflowers, which to my eyes are hardly purple, more a shade of pink. In this flower the radiant orange "cone" is serenaded by pink radiating petals—evidence to anyone that orange and pink are aptly suited to each other.

Even when a flower petal appears to be a single color, if you look closely you will discover the subtle gradations ranging from darker hues near the center of the flower to the lightest toward the end of the petal. This gradient from dark to light can be applied directly to your garden. Once again, nature is the best teacher; we need only to be observant and she will reveal her color secrets.

Using Seasonal Color

Gertrude Jekyll, the great doyen of English flower gardening who is responsible for much of the work done in garden color theory, created gardens with contrasting hues next to one another. For instance, a purple-themed garden would be immediately juxtaposed with one in hot orange. This extreme shift from one color to its complement heightens the visual experience, intensifying its brilliance.

Today few of us have the luxury of creating several large garden rooms each dedicated to a single color plan. We have to adapt our planting schemes to the realities of limited space, time, and resources. However, you can use seasonal color shifts in a single flower bed to develop different palettes. In the spring, you might create a quiet theme in soft pastels with bulbs and flowering shrubs. During summer, you can then shift the colors to bright yellows and reds with perennials and annuals. By fall, the colors of chrysanthemums and late-blooming salvias can bring seasonal shades to the same area.

Within these seasonal color schemes, use a range of the same color en masse. Large swaths of color always have more visual impact. Combining three slightly different flower shades of the same color in a mass planting is more effective than using a single color. For instance, if you are planting blue pansies, mix one part dark blue to two parts medium blue to one part light blue. The subtle variation in the hues makes the composition more alive and visually interesting.

Another seasonal color technique is to play off the color of a tree or shrub that takes center stage during certain times of the year. If there is an explosion of pink from a flowering crab apple in your garden, the surrounding beds should complement and support that feature. In the fall, the focus may be on a golden-hued sugar maple. Look for opportunities in your landscape to build on what you have.

In every season you can create endless color combinations from the myriad of blooms and foliage available to you. As you begin your color scheme, start in one room of the garden with a single color family and develop a color palette that matches the function of the room with your own color preferences and style.

Color and Garden Furnishings

As you select furnishings for your garden rooms, keep in mind that the style of the furnishing in combination with its color will have an impact on the expression of your style. For instance, a classic garden bench can either blend quietly into the fabric of the garden as weathered wood or stand out if painted a bright color, serving as more of a focal point.

You can really have some fun with color and garden furnishings and let your personality shine through. Many of the same color theories that apply to using color with plants hold true for your garden furnishings. Bright primary colors, particularly reds, give the garden the sense of being smaller because they appear to jump forward. Softer pastels and blues will create the illusion of greater depth.

Complementary color schemes will heighten the intensity of the hues as well as visual interest. If your garden comprises pale yellows and buttery creams, a pair of dull, chalky blue Adirondack chairs on the lawn might be just the right touch. A more contemporary garden of various shades of green can be set off with an ensemble of Chinese red chairs and a bench. If you are not that adventurous, a more subtle and safe approach may better suit you. Work with the color of tree trunks. Grungy greens and gray are neutral hues that create an unobtrusive presence in the garden. Lichens and mosses are also wonderful sources of color inspiration.

Terra-cotta and concrete containers are popular choices for "furnishing" areas of garden rooms. You can modify the color of terra-cotta containers if the bright orange clay does not harmonize with the color palette of the space. A light wash of old-fashioned milk paint can help. Dull greens and taupe applied with a light hand can neutralize the intense orange of new terra-cotta. Glazing is another way to add and modify color in the garden. Transform an ordinary strawberry jar into a more sophisticated version of itself with a dark green, blue, or even black glaze. The dark, hard, glossy finish is an attractive juxtaposition for softer glaucous leaves of sedums and sempervivums.

"Aging" new concrete can go a long way to help these objects settle into the garden. Toning down the edge of newness for these often "too white" accents can be achieved in a number of ways. Applying the time-honored method of sheep manure and buttermilk is as unattractive as it sounds, but it does work and helps to establish an environment for algae and mosses to grow in. But I prefer to find a soft green-gray latex paint and apply it to the concrete. Then I rub the object all over with handfuls of grass. This simple technique gives the concrete an instant aged appearance.

Texture, Pattern, and Rhythm

As you think about ways to add depth and character to your garden home, your instinct may be to head for the nearest garden center to gather up a carload of blooming flowers to "paint" the rooms with color. There is no doubt that when a garden is in full flower the impact of all those colorful blossoms is hard to ignore. But before that happens it is important to keep in mind that through the seasons, flowers bloom and fade, leaving a garden's shrubs and trees to provide dimension and interest for the rest of the year. As gardeners come to recognize this fact, they develop a more discerning eye and look carefully at a plant's foliage as well as its flowers.

The role that texture, pattern, and rhythm play in the look of a well-designed garden is often overlooked and underrated. Color from flowers alone cannot sustain interest—you must weave it together with other elements. Creating a visually interesting framework of contrasting textures, patterns, and rhythms that supports the color scheme is the best approach.

Shrubs can help you interlace texture and color. Since shrubs are the mainstay, the real workhorses of the garden, they can introduce longer-lasting color into your garden and provide interesting textures. In my garden, maroon barberry shrubs, purple smoke trees, and old-fashioned shrub roses serve as long-term players in one area of my garden. Over this foundation of color and texture, I then add complementary seasonal colors with bulbs and annuals in pockets around them.

Apart from the visual strength this adds to a garden, there are also very practical reasons to adopt this strategy—it saves time and money. Shrubs fill important areas in the flower beds, places that you will not have to replant each spring with annuals. This reduces the amount of work and financial resources you would have to spend filling the entire bed with seasonal flowers.

Blooming shrubs add their own color to the mix, but you need to consider how the foliage will look once the flowers fade. In spring, many of my garden center customers become so dazzled by the various colors of the blooming azaleas that they do not even notice they are buying plants with nearly identical foliage. After the spring blooms faded, they are left with a border of plants that all look the same.

All too frequently there is a monotonous textural consistency to plants around our homes. Certain varieties of azaleas, along other tiny flowered or oval "mouse-ear" leaves, such as boxwood, Japanese hollies, yaupon holly, and serissa, have similar textural appearance. The eye is quickly bored by the same leaf texture over and over without variation to stimulate interest. You will find it more appealing when refined delicate plants are set next to those with larger, coarser foliage and blooms, as well as the plumes of grasses. This same rule applies to flowers.

The more extreme the textural contrast between the plants, the more visually interesting they are to look at. Some beautiful combinations are the soft plumes of ornamental grasses against the broad leaves of canna; feathery bronze fennel combined with stalks of Brussels sprouts; lacy ferns and wide-leafed hostas. Each plant is appreciated even more when it is paired with contrasting textures.

A diversity of surface treatments can also be layered into your garden rooms with other features. Pathways, ground covers, fences, buildings, and other elements of decoration can be opportunities to infuse rich and varied textural interest into your garden rooms.

Pattern, the second component of principle 8, will help you add your own personal "stamp" to each room. One method is to choose a symbol, emblem, or insignia that you can use throughout your garden rooms. Look for unique motifs to repeat in various places.

I chose an X design from a transom window originally above a door salvaged for the toolshed. The pattern was repeated in several areas—in the layout of the parterre garden, as part of the gate, in the vegetable garden, and in the design of the mixed entry pad. This recurring symbol adds a personal signature throughout the garden.

Some gardeners seem to have an innate flair for dealing with pattern and, for that matter, all the elements of design. Known for creating the English country house look, the interior designer Nancy Lancaster had an equally impressive eye for the garden. My visits to her home at Little Hasely Court in England always left me spellbound by the way she could put things together. Her planting schemes were bold and dynamic—projecting the same strong sense of style and confidence found in her interior designs. There was a richness of texture, pattern, and rhythm throughout her garden.

Within her walled garden area, she laid out the pattern of a wagon wheel. The design was outlined in boxwoods, punctuated with weeping mulberries, and filled with a tumble of roses, perennials, and annuals. Nancy recognized that a formal, clearly designed pattern is to a garden what bone structure is to a face—once you have it in place, you can add the curves and colors of the "flesh." "Bone structure lasts longer, a stronger layout, then the softness of informal planting," she once said. Hasely was proof of that.

Before choosing a motif, think about how you intend to apply it. As you work through various scenarios you will discover that simpler designs are easier to work with. Elaborate patterns do not seem to wear as well and are not as adaptable as a more straightforward design.

Fences in wood and metal can add delightfully rich patterns to a garden. Look for ways to alter standard fencing material to infuse more imaginative designs: Add finials to the posts, apply trim or molding to the fence rails, or personalize the gates.

Another source of pattern can be found in plants. You need only look at the variegation found in the leaves of *Heuchera* 'Silver Scrolls' or *Lamium* 'White Nancy' to see how the interplay of white and green can produce a captivating effect.

To employ variegated foliage effectively, add them with a measured hand. As in our homes, too much pattern in too little space can be overwhelming. And just as you would not mix plaids with paisleys, rarely will juxtaposing one variegated leaf against another create a successful result. Instead use them as appointments to lighten a dark corner or to mediate contrasting colors.

Just as a painting, swatch of fabric, or wallpaper can serve as a springboard for colors in a particular room of your home, some of the more exuberant tropical plants such as cannas, dracenias, and coleus offer bold and gutsy patterns for inspired decorating schemes in your garden rooms. And don't forget about the opportunities to add pattern in your gardens through the use of pillows, tablecloths, and curtains. Today there are more fabrics available that are weatherproof, allowing you to extend the feel of the inside of your home into the garden. These creature comforts not only make living in your gardens more comfortable and inviting, but also serve as accents to add panache.

The third component of principle 8 is rhythm, a powerful element that can be felt, but is not always consciously recognized, in a garden's design. Consider the experience of listening to a song. Often, as we hum along to one of our favorite tunes, we do not even notice the music's beat, because we are taken by the lyrics or the melody, but without that percussive presence, the song would feel incomplete. The same holds true for a garden. Without a sense of rhythm in a garden's design, the area can seem like a rambling series of notes trying to find a tune.

As you begin to think about ways to add this element to your garden rooms, a good place to start is to notice how rhythm is woven into the scenes around you. It is found in the regular spacing of windows on a house, columns on a porch, fence posts along a field, or trees lining a driveway.

In your garden, you can achieve a sense of rhythm by equally spacing three or more objects (either all the same or similar in look or style) along a wall, up the steps, through a border, or next to a path. It is the objects themselves and the space around them that conspire to create a rhythmic presence. As you begin to experiment, you will find that bolder objects carry a greater sense of continuity, regularity, and therefore a stronger rhythm. For example, several oversize Italian

terra-cotta pots filled with large boxwood balls can be used to create height and establish rhythm in a flower border. The placement of three to five evenly spaced containers (depending on the length of the border) is a simple device for establishing a prominent cadence. The same evergreen boxwoods planted directly in the bed can also be used to anchor a sweeping display of daylilies. The regular presence of these forms gives the garden visual weight and stability.

You can also use distinctively shaped plants placed at regular intervals to achieve the same goal. Cone-shaped evergreens such as holly, yew, and juniper make strong silhouettes in the winter garden. If you have a fence or hedge, try arranging tall, columnar, or fastigiate forms such as arborvitae, chamaecyparis (false cypress), or juniper behind the border to create both a sense of rhythm and to give the area greater depth.

A question that often comes up is "What guidelines should I follow in spacing objects?" A good rule of thumb to follow is, the more objects you have to work with, the greater the distance between them should be. For instance, three containers usually look best when placed close to one another, but the same spacing would not work with seven. Placing objects too close together can result in a congested or monotonous appearance. Negative space between objects is as important as the objects themselves.

To determine the spacing between objects, use the object itself as a gauge. If, for example, you are using a series of matching containers, measure one at its widest point and use a multiple of that dimension for the spacing in between. Decide if you want the distance between the containers to be half, one, or two times that dimension. This guide will help you maintain a sense of proportion between the objects. From there, stand back and make "intuitive adjustments" by shifting the containers slightly one way or another until the spacing feels right to you.

When placing a series of objects, remember that their spacing helps to suggest the pace of the rhythm. It has a psychological effect on our movement through the space. For example, the spacing of columnar evergreens along a path may influence your stride as you walk down a path. Long stretches between each tree invite a more relaxed and leisurely walk, while arranging them closer to one another might encourage you to quicken the pace.

You can also bring a "wave" of rhythm into a garden room with undulating curves in a line of shrubs. A striking example can be found at Chatsworth, a magnificent house and garden in Derbyshire, England, that date from the seventeenth century. The garden has gone through several awe-inspiring transformations over the centuries, but the Duchess of Devonshire is a keen gardener, and she has added vitality to the landscape with several of her own touches. In one area, a pair of serpentine beech hedges transforms a pathway into a flowing, sensuous experience. In this case, rhythm plays a large role in inviting you into the garden.

While few of us have grand estates the size of Chatsworth, we can learn from its example. You can apply this serpentine motif on a scale that fits your garden. Low hedge borders or even annuals can make a stylish turn when laid out in an undulating line. Any number of low border shrubs suited to shearing can be used in this way. Annuals with a dense compact form, such as fibrous begonias, are a colorful twist on this idea.

Adding Abundance

Abundance is one of my favorite elements of design. As an avid collector who is always trying to find ways to squeeze more plants into my garden rooms, I wholeheartedly embrace this idea. However, to use this principle effectively: It does not mean you should buy lots of plants. Abundance is best articulated by repeating plants that already exist in your garden. This approach is a sure way to bring order rather than chaos to a space.

Often when I work with clients, they expect that I will introduce them to an entirely new palette of plants —rare, unknown discoveries that will somehow magically transform their gardens. More often than not, this does not happen. Instead, we build on what already exists and is successful so that their gardens begin to feel rich and full.

Organizing scattered plants that are lost as individual and random elements into large drifts helps pull a space together. The same guideline used for color applies here—if you use bold splashes to make a stronger visual impact, your garden rooms will feel lush.

First, group and consolidate your plants to create reorganized masses before you introduce new varieties. Strive to create natural drifts by planting in odd numbers of three, five, and seven plants. Even-numbered arrangements tend to work better in more formal settings where symmetry is desired.

When creating drifts in your garden it is important not to overdo it. Too much of the same thing looks rote and corporate, lacking in imagination and creativity. The composition becomes uninteresting to the point that it is rarely compelling. If you plant a large drift of a single flower as a focal point in the garden, avoid using that same flower in a similar way as an accent in other areas of the garden.

While too much of the same thing can look excessive, the consistent use of certain "workhorse" plants in the framework of your rooms provides a sense of continuity in the garden. There are usually a handful of trees, shrubs, and perennials that are hardy, low-maintenance plants that you can rely on to establish the bones of your garden rooms. The broad and generous use of such plants in the framework brings order and harmony to the overall scheme. With these plants in place, you are free to appoint the garden with a range of accent plantings without disrupting the unity of the overall composition.

Many gardeners are hesitant to cut flowers in their gardens for fear of ruining their displays. Planting with a generous hand can solve this. In the fall, plant extra tulip bulbs so you will have plenty to gather for spring bouquets or to share with friends. Likewise, when sowing summer annuals such as zinnias, cosmos, and celosia, sow enough seeds so that a portion of the blooms can be used as cut flowers. Buying extra bulbs to fill pots for the house is a good way to bring the abundance of nature indoors. The fragrant oriental lilies, hyacinths, and pineapple lilies are good choices.

You can prolong a plant's visual display by staggering bloom times. This not only extends the season of bloom, but it also allows you to get the most out of your bed space. To stagger bloom times, choose early-, mid-, and late-flowering varieties of a single plant, making sure that the colors of each variety will complement one another, as there will be some overlap. Daffodils, tulips, daylilies, peonies, and iris are all examples of flowers that offer a range of bloom times.

One of the greatest joys of gardening is sharing the abundance. Growing enough to offer others

SOME HARDY VOLUNTEERS

Lunaria annua (money plant)

Digitalis purpurea (biennial foxglove)

Viola tricolor (Johnny-jump-up)

Cosmos bipinnatus

Celosia cristata (cockscomb)

Nicotiana sylvestris (flowering tobacco)

Consolida ambigua (larkspur)

Petunia hybrida (old-fashioned petunias)

Cleome hasslerana (spider flower)

Lupinus species (bluebonnets)

Daucus carota (Queen Anne's lace)

Centaurea cyanus (cornflowers)

Poppies

Nigella damascena (love-in-a-mist)

Verbena bonariensis

SHAPE	FORM	EXAMPLES
Round	Dense balls of petals. The blooms tend to have a heavy, solid appearance that is dramatic and commands attention. Others have a distinct spherical shape that is more ethereal.	Summer phlox, peonies, hydrangeas, geraniums, alliums
Umbel	Flat-topped and tiered. These flowers have the appearance of plateaus or umbrellas.	Yarrow, fennel, dill, angelica, Queen Anne's lace, *Sedum spectabile*, lace-cap hydrangea
Mounding	Low, broad, spreading crowns of foliage that form a domelike sphere. The foliage is often more compelling than the flower.	Dianthus (pinks), *Artemisia* 'Powis Castle', santolina, geranium, hosta
Spiky	Bold, vertical growth and blooms that seem to erupt from the ground. Effective in both front and back of the border.	Liatris, eremurus, lupines, baptisia, ligularia, echiums, foxtail lily
Frothy	Foaming waves of flowers and foliage that stay low to the ground but rise up with an ethereal and airy feeling.	Catnip, foam flower, heuchera, saxifrage, strawberry begonia
Shooting stars	Small clusters of flowers frequently suspended in space on delicate stems. They add a subtle vertical dimension to the garden and are not as delicate as they appear.	Angels'-fishing-rods (*Dierama*), *Verbena bonariensis*
Grasslike	Bold linear foliage. Vertical and upright. Fine- to medium-textured leaves arranged as part of a distinct silhouette.	Iris, yucca, New Zealand flax (Phornium), agave, crinums, agapanthus, amaryllis, crocosmia, daylily, ornamental grasses
Ethereal	Plants with delicate, weightless appearance. They frequently benefit from being placed in front of a simple background to keep them from disappearing.	Gaura, some New England asters, Russian sage, baby's breath, lavender, *Verbena rigida*, *Coreopsis* 'Moonbeam'
Plumelike	Feathery, delicate blooms that appear to defy gravity.	Astilbe, aruncus, ghost plant (*Artemisia lactiflora*), plume poppy (*Macleaya cordata*), filipendula
Bold architectural	Striking, dramatic plant forms that can serve as a focal point. Typically, less is more with these attention-getters. Site them where their bold lines can be appreciated.	Acanthus, cardoon, artichoke, Scotch thistle (*Onopordum*), gunnera
Candelabra	Several upright branching blooms having the appearance of a candelabrum.	Century plant (*Agave americana*), common turkscap lily (*Lilium superbum*), primrose (*Primula pulverulenta*)

is especially easy to do in the vegetable garden. Even if you have a limited amount of space, there are some simple steps you can take to maximize your harvest. When sowing lettuce, stagger your planting times every ten days to two weeks. This will give you a constant supply of leafy greens until hot weather sets in. Another tip is to plant a row of seeds at the same time you plant young seedlings. I have found this method works well with broccoli, lettuce, peas, carrots, and radishes. You can use the same technique with warm-season vegetables as well.

Shape and Form of Flowers

Another influence in creating a certain personal style within your garden rooms is working with the abundance of shapes and forms of flowers. Some people have strong preferences. One of my friends doesn't like lilies, or any flower with a lily-like bloom, because the form reminds her of funerals. Another dislikes hydrangeas, so no bloom of that shape will do—including viburnums and even alliums—because he finds the round sphere shape unappealing.

How do we form such strong preferences? After I suggested underplanting a tree with white caladiums to lighten a somber shady area, a client turned to me and, with one hand on her hip firmly stated, "Caladiums? No way, honey, they remind me of bell-bottomed pants! I've been there and done that and once is enough for

me!" Clearly the shape of the large single leaf brought with it a reminder of another time she did not wish to revisit. Apparently plants, like people, have innate personalities and not all are compatible.

An experienced floral arranger gave me one of my best lessons on how to create successful combinations of plants in containers based on their shapes and forms. Her simple but effective suggestion is to start in the back with tall and spiky plants, such as delphiniums, foxgloves, or liatris. Then add round and bold plant forms in the middle, such as hydrangeas, tulips, or peonies, with something light and ethereal, like asters, baby's breath, or beauty bush, to fill in. The finishing touch is to have ivy or another climber cascade down the sides.

I have tried a similar formula for outdoor containers, using tall and spiky plants, such as dracaenas, cannas, and iris, in the middle of the container. The surrounding area is filled with full-bodied shapes, such as heliotropes and geraniums. To cascade down the sides of the container, I have used ivies, petunias, and sweet potato vines. The forms offer enough contrast so that the arrangement is interesting whether the plants bloom or not.

This same method of using shapes applies to the broader scale of our gardens. The juxtaposition of contrasting forms can be carried into the landscape to create more interesting compositions. As a simple exercise, walk out into your garden; try to visualize your accent plants as shapes; look for those that are cascading, upright, and round.

Whimsy

The sheer delight of a garden can transport us to a childlike state of wonder and excitement, preparing us to experience fantasy and whimsy. It is a place where we can disconnect from the person society tells us we should be; there, we can find who we were meant to be —the natural self—rediscovered in a state of nature.

While it might seem odd to designate whimsy as a

principle of design, I cannot imagine a garden without this element. Gardens should be purposefully created as places to give us pleasure and make us happy. They should have special areas reserved for joy and self-discovery, places where fantasy can be played out. Spending more time in nature through our gardens draws us closer to that wellspring of creative life energy.

Carrying an element of whimsy from one room to the next is a way to create a thread of continuity through your garden home. One idea is to place a series of clues to a riddle at various stations along a path. As you traverse through the garden, the riddle is solved. This idea can be applied to any theme.

Consider using a series of mirrors and reflective surfaces. Mirrors add an illusion of depth, as well as an element of surprise. Maybe you have a collection of weather vanes or whirligigs that come to life with a breeze. Rather than grouping them together, as you might treat a collection indoors, place them throughout your garden. Repeated use of like objects reinforces a whimsical spirit.

Certain elements in a garden lend themselves to humorous touches and can add a lighthearted feel. Look to water features, sculptures, gates, and shelters for your pets as places to design a whimsical theme.

The simplest things—plants with amusing or unusual names or a funny-looking birdhouse—can incite a smile and put us in touch with our own creativity. Having some fun with ordinary plants in the garden always captures our imagination. Topiary with all its whimsical qualities can add a jolt of humor. Standard topiary can be used as punctuation or, when used in a series, to create a sense of rhythm. More fanciful shapes become elements of surprise as you turn a corner and see a peacock clipped from a hedge, or enter a garden room to find a whimsical form waiting to delight you. Such shapes are better appreciated if displayed against a plain background such as the sky or a wall or hedge of a contrasting color.

One of my favorite forms of whimsy is serendipity, when Mother Nature creates her own design through her hardy volunteers. These are plants that freely reseed themselves from last year's blooms or are delivered to the garden by the wind or a bird. Allowing plants to come up randomly throughout the garden may be a hard concept to accept if you lean toward being a tidy gardener, but as Thomas Church said, "Absolute perfection, like complete consistency, can be dull."

Hardy volunteers bring a carefree quality to the garden that is not easily produced by our hands. There is an unexpected pleasure in discovering a patch of cornflowers, poppies, or violas that springs up on its own. I remember a bed of old-fashioned petunias at my aunt's house that merrily reseeded every year under an apple tree. They were a sweet-smelling profusion of pink blooms. Even though their appearance became almost expected, we were always astonished and delighted to see them each spring.

If you would like to encourage hardy volunteers to grow in your garden, there are a few things you can do to help. Allow some of your plants to go to seed, rather than deadheading them after the flowers fade. As you begin your fall garden cleanup, collect and scatter the seed pods from your favorite annuals. In areas where you want the plants to reseed, avoid heavy mulching

and the use of pre-emergent herbicides, as these are the mortal enemies of young seedlings.

There are several techniques for altering the natural forms of plants to add a sense of fun and whimsy to your garden design. Plants shaped in these humorous ways stand out and attract attention. These techniques traditionally are employed in more formal landscapes, but you may want to use them in your garden to create a distinctive splash. Incorporating shaped plants in informal gardens is like placing a fine piece of porcelain in a rustic situation. The juxtaposition of forms is interesting.

Woody plants grown or trained in a "standard" take on the classic lollipop form, which is made distinct by carefully manicuring the top into a round ball supported by a single trunk. These distinguishing accents can be used in the garden to create contrast, establish rhythm, provide punctuation, and introduce some fun.

My friend Rosemary Verey grew several burning bushes as standards lined up along a central pathway in her garden at Barnsley House in Cirencester, Gloucestershire, England. While we were looking at them, she told me with a wry grin that she was encouraging the nurserymen to call them "Great Balls of Fire." Most often a tree rose, lollipop ivy tree, holly, or boxwood is grown in a standard form, but seeing euonymus shaped in this surprising way made me realize that there was no limit to the plants that could be grown in this fashion.

In pleaching, a row of closely planted trees or shrubs is sheared to create a thin wall of foliage. The limbs of the plants become interlaced or plaited together into a single plane. Pleaching is practiced commonly in Europe but is gaining popularity in the United States.

Espalier is a method similar to pleaching in that you are pruning the limbs to grow in a single plane. Historically, espaliered trees were grown against walls to promote flower and fruit production. Use espaliered plants when bed space is limited and gardens require the cre-

ative use of vertical space. You should be aware that this technique, like growing bonsai, requires time and patience. Certain gardeners seem to be better suited to this artistic style than others. It requires vigilance, discipline, and an artful approach to be successful.

Keeping Whimsy in Balance

As you add your sense of fun and creativity to your garden decor, it is important to maintain a balance between whimsy and over-the-top wacky. Statues, ironwork forms, three-dimensional carvings, and sculpture can all add unique and arresting elements to a garden. But to make them memorable, use some measure of restraint.

I recall visiting one garden in which the homeowner's passion for sculpture became a distraction rather than an attractive feature. It looked as though he had been taken advantage of by a traveling salesman and an entire truckload of concrete yard art had been unloaded in the garden. Swan planters, a copy of Michelangelo's *David*, classical nudes, and the Seven Dwarfs—all of the overused, hackneyed pieces we see time and time again. It was quite a sight to behold.

These features, used to excess, had become a distraction instead of the harmonizing presence in the garden as they were originally intended to be. It was a perfectly beautiful garden, full of interesting plants, walkways, fish ponds—a nicely designed space, but, sadly, upstaged by too much whimsy. As we were leaving, a friend shared an analogy with me. "Gardens and garden embellishments are similar to a woman's clothing and her accessories. They should never overpower, but always try to strike just the right balance, and what we just saw was one overly bejeweled woman!"

Mystery

Adding a sense of mystery to a garden is often one of the most overlooked elements. Things that are hidden from view, secretive and obscure, are often the most exhilarating and thrilling to us. So how can we integrate such an elusive and abstract idea into the fabric of our gardens? Many of the principles outlined in this book will help you set up this game of seduction. When you create enclosures, you reveal areas of your garden bit by bit rather than all at once. This establishes opportunities for mystery. As one room leads us into the next, the entire picture is never fully revealed. You control the garden experience, offering glimpses here and there, luring the visitor into one space, then through hedges, screens, under vines, and around curving paths. A simple hedge with an opening cut through it can become a device that stirs intrigue and mystery in your garden.

Another simple way to add mystery to your garden is in how you lay out your paths. The slightest curve can conceal the ultimate destination, enticing the visitor to areas beyond. The bend of a path is often a good position for a clump of shrubs or a drift of ornamental grasses. Concealing paths with points of transition such as gates, arbors, or a flight of steps will help hold the garden visitor in suspense.

The elements of earth, wind, water, and fire offer their own sense of mystery, especially water. I always look for ways to include water in my designs. Like an oasis, it draws us closer, arousing a feeling of expectation. Since water is the source of all life, it carries with it a restorative power as a symbol of renewal.

Water can be used in many ways on any scale—from large pools to wall fountains. Depending on the application, it can serve as a subtle accent or as part of the floor in a garden room. It's the perfect way to capture the splendor of the sky. The life-giving water that brings magic to the garden in so many ways can also reflect the heavens at your feet. A simple circle of water—a round, shimmering mirror of constant change—adds a restorative quality to the garden room that the most technologically advanced gadgetry could never achieve.

Water appeals to each of our senses, soothing us as we sit and listen to its movement. To achieve this effect, select pools that are large enough to accommodate a few water plants and designed to produce the sound of water. You may find that you are less interested in an impressive show of hydraulics than in a pleasant, relaxing flow, not too loud but clearly audible.

The wind also adds a mysterious quality to garden rooms. You can capture its elusive nature by adding plants that are "wind catchers." Soft and fluid, these trees, shrubs, and flowers will dance and sway in the breeze, enlivening the garden with their movements. Wind chimes also announce the wind's arrival. Melodic songs give puffs of air a voice and add another dimension to the garden. The distant sound of wind chimes gives us pause to stop and listen.

Fire is another source of mystery in the garden, prompting memories of bonfires, summer camps, and hayrides. The glow of a fire at night is a source of light and shadows that many find alluring. Whether in the form of a fire ring, a freestanding outdoor fireplace, or a barbecue area, this primal element offers an exciting and mysterious glow to the garden.

So much about bringing a sense of mystery into the garden is about not revealing the entire picture but leaving something for our imagination to ponder. By holding back the full experience and using the unknown as a tool, we set into motion a heightened sense of wonder and surprise in our gardens.

Finding Your Garden's Place in Time

While it may be easy to identify the year in which a particular style of clothing or decor was popular, most of us would find it more challenging to assign a time to garden designs of yesterday. This uncertainty often results in a confusing blend of outdoor styles. Although few of us would consider mixing an Elizabethan collar with a tube top, we seem unconcerned about combining an ornate wrought-iron bench with a rustic picket fence.

As you decorate your garden rooms, it is important for you to acknowledge your home's place in time and make an effort to match your garden rooms' furnishings with that period and style.

Whether you live in a new or an old house, your home's architecture and interior design reflect a time period in which certain elements were signatures of the day. When you recognize those features and echo them in the spirit of your garden rooms, you create a harmonious blend that unifies the house and garden into a cohesive whole.

If you live in a house that has some history, it can be fun and enlightening to do a little research on its past. Neighbors or historical societies may have early photographs of your home. By studying these pictures, you can piece together ideas for fences, plantings, or porches that you might want to add to your garden rooms to honor the spirit of those early days. You will be surprised at how many things you can pick up and use as a springboard for inspiration.

I encourage you to look for old copies of magazines from your home's time period to study the pictures for ideas. Libraries or the Internet are useful resources in your treasure hunt. You may discover all kinds of examples, from various types of outdoor furniture to heritage plants and colors, that will capture the feel of the time and give your garden a stronger sense of place.

Even if you have a new home, most are designed to be reminiscent of a certain style. But whatever the model—Colonial or contemporary—the idea is to study and reflect those period details in the garden. Many homes in the suburbs can have a cookie-cutter feel; each house looks like all the others on the street. But when the garden design matches the period and style of the house, it feels congruent with the dwelling.

Most houses offer some type of architectural style to respond to, but if you prefer not to underscore that connection, try to work with some redeemable material that is present in the structure, such as brick or stone, to create harmony. One client who lived in a brick ranch-style home chose not to go to the expense of building a brick wall entirely around her garden room; instead, she decided to create a panel of brick, place a bench in front of it with trees on each side, and use hedges to enclose the rest of the area. The panel of brick was just enough to work off the house so that it felt like an extension without going overboard with that material. The details in the panel reflected the style and time of the house, connecting them together.

As you select benches, containers, fountains, trellises, and furnishings for your garden rooms, try to match their style with the time period of your home's interior and exterior. Just as with color, if you want to be safe, you can choose one of the "neutral" designs that seem to harmonize with all periods. These pieces are "timeless" in their simplicity and classic design. It is always interesting to see an object from the eighteenth or nineteenth century fitting comfortably into a modern garden. Those that work best are round spheres and simple geometric forms that are elegant in their sophistication. A simple teak bench with a slight camel back and turned legs is a more timeless choice than a cast aluminum bench adorned with tired decorative motifs. The best advice here is to stay away from objects that are mass-produced and have become clichés.

If you become a discerning buyer, you will add embellishments with enduring beauty to your garden. Whether you plan on developing your garden for only a few years or many, you are creating a legacy that will be passed on. You should make sure it is a lasting one.

If you are selecting statuary, original period pieces are best. The next best choice is garden ornaments with simple, unpretentious forms. The human form is often difficult to use in a garden unless the sculpture is an original. Stamped-out figures often appear inferior. Some manufactured objects blend easily into the gar-

den, however. Ball finials, troughs, pedestals, and simple concrete containers can be interesting and tasteful additions. Just be careful that your selection matches your home. Large, classic Greek statuary suggests a grand home and garden—make sure the images agree.

An eclectic style of decorating is a popular look, both inside and out. But to really make it work, you need guts and some guidelines. It is a common mistake to gather random objects and assume that they will somehow come together and produce a satisfying composition. Without a thread of continuity tying all of the objects together, the results are often more chaotic than convincing. As we find when working with textures and colors, a juxtaposition of contrasting objects can set off and heighten the visual effect. Objects that are similar in form are less jarring to the eye when grouped together and appear more harmonious. Garden ornaments, like furnishings in our homes, bring with them cultural and historical associations that should be recognized; each reflects a certain ethos determined by time and place.

For instance, if you mix the simple, clean lines of an eighteenth-century furnishing with a highly ornamental Victorian piece, it is unlikely that you will achieve any visual congruity. Perhaps an object that is stark and modern would be a more compatible match. If you keep the lines of the objects similar, you will capture the spirit of any ages you mix without having them clash. Simply keep the objects aesthetically compatible in the space where they are being viewed.

Having said all that, at the end of the day, creating your own style is more about doing what you want to do, and surrounding yourself with things that are pleasing and comforting to you, than just duplicating other styles. I offer these suggestions only as guides—if you find something that speaks to you, by all means, you should have it.

We tend to want to speed up time—desiring a garden that is fully grown and mature soon after it is planted. We can't wait until that special sapling grows to fill a blank corner, a group of tiny shrubs fills in to form a drift of foliage, or the bulbs we planted in the fall come up and bloom in the spring. The garden fills us with anticipation and hope for the future.

To help satisfy that urge, you can use fast-growers for immediate gratification while allowing the slower-growing structure or bones to mature. It's important not to compromise your selection for the framework of the garden for something that will grow fast and satisfy the moment. Choose plants with the long term in mind.

I recall how fast-growing plants helped a young client with her first garden. When I arrived to have a look, it was clear that she had just moved into her 1920s bungalow—boxes and packing paper were strewn across the porch. I thought to myself, "How could she possibly find the time to focus on a garden?"

Despite the move, she was brimming with enthusiasm about getting started. She was thrilled, and rightfully so, as her new home was a charming place rife with potential. I was concerned about her intention to launch into a full-scale gardening project so soon, but I could tell that she felt pressed to plant something, anything. It was late May, and as she saw it, time was getting away from her, and it would soon be too late.

I attempted to advise her that her first step should be waiting one full year to give her time to observe the garden in each season before making major improvements. That was not what she wanted to hear, so we tried to reach a compromise. I encouraged her to think about the past and recall a happy memory she held about a garden. Without hesitation she said, "It's my grandmother's garden and her beautiful zinnias."

Since zinnias are fast-growing, carefree annuals, I knew we had come up with a solution that would satisfy her desire to plant something that would give her quick results. The bed of cheerful zinnias did indeed bring her lots of joy that first year. This simple exercise revived the happy memory of her grandmother's garden and at the same time helped ease her anxiety. Equally important, it was a way of giving her more time to become familiar with a new garden so that the decisions she made in the future would be ones she could live with for a long time.

Part of living in the present is to embrace the best of what is available today. Our lives, as well as our gardens, are dictated by the time we live in, and we should respond to both its opportunities and its challenges. The garden world has been flooded with all kinds of inventions and devices that help make gardening less of a chore and more of a delight. Labor-saving equipment and supplies that ease the drudgery of gardening have been a real blessing. At the same time, some of these solutions have created new sets of problems, especially for the environment. Becoming less dependent on toxic approaches previous generations used to manage pests and plant diseases will help all of us live in a healthier and more sustainable way.

Become more conscious about reducing your use of nonrenewable resources such as gas and oil. Choose to add more flower beds and decrease the size of your lawn. Planting ground covers is another alternative. Making plant selections that are better suited for periods of drought and using water-saving devices help us become "greener" citizens. As we look ahead into the future, I hope there will be more time for us to spend with nature in our gardens. By creating a garden home,

you will surround yourself with living spaces that invite that connection. It has been my pleasure to meet and to work with people who are close to the earth. Both they and their gardens seem to be the better for it.

Over the years, the experiences that have shaped my approach to garden design have been broad and diverse. My agrarian background and love of the land, as well as my studies abroad, where I encountered so many exceptional gardens, have influenced my views and my relationship to nature.

These experiences have developed in me a strong need to be connected to the earth and to have a place to cultivate and call my own. This seems to be a feeling shared by most gardeners I encounter—by growing things in the soil, we literally become more grounded. As we nurture our gardens, they in turn nurture us.

With my own garden as a place to experiment and apply my ideas, I found fertile ground for the concept of creating a garden home. As I stretched the boundaries of a traditional garden into outdoor "living" rooms, I became excited in the way these areas could help homeowners rediscover their connection to the earth. Each garden I designed allowed me to test the effectiveness of the twelve principles in developing these uniquely personal spaces. Throughout this process, I have always come back to the principles as helpful guides to organize my thoughts and provide the essential tools as I assist others in designing their garden homes.

My hope is that this book will be helpful to you by being both general enough to be timeless and versatile enough to grow with your abilities and aspirations as you weave together the rich fabric of your garden rooms. I also invite you to visit other gardens with these principles in mind. Use them to develop a discerning eye so you can create a garden home full of beauty and wonder. May you find happiness in your endeavor and enjoy the feeling, as Willa Cather has written, to "be dissolved into something complete and great."

ACKNOWLEDGMENTS

This book distills a lifetime of inspiration, observations, and experience, and like a garden, it has required the talents and dedication of many people to create. So with gratitude I thank all of those who, in countless ways, contributed to this book.

I am most grateful to Betsy Lyman, for without her tireless enthusiasm, confidence, and enormous practical help this book would have never been written. Her perseverance, dedication, and creative spirit kept the manuscript on course. This book would be nothing without Jane Colclasure's extraordinary photographs. Each time she presented a new set of images, I found myself swept up by their richness and beauty. My thanks to Mary Ellen Pyle, whose countless hours of coordinating and organizing photography and text helped to craft the book into something useful and comprehensible. I thank Ward Lile for generously sharing his thoughts and opinions about the text, and for making me laugh while in the throes of writing.

I am especially fortunate to have the vision and skill of my editor, Lauren Shakely, whose clarity and insights helped to shape and direct the manuscript. A special thanks is due to all those at Clarkson Potter who believed in the project from the beginning and carried it through with enthusiasm, especially Mark McCauslin, Joan Denman, and Caitlin Israel. Likewise, I am grateful for the creative art direction of Marysarah Quinn and Jennifer Napier, who so artfully brought this book to life through such a beautiful marriage of text, photography, and drawings.

I thank all of my friends and clients who have allowed me the pleasure of creating gardens with them over the years, and especially those who have opened their homes and gardens for the creation of this book; each person and place has played a special role in developing the ideas found within this text: Robert and Gaye Anderson, Overton and Kay Anderson, Mark and Kim Brockinton, Robert Brown and Charlotte Banks Brown, Rick and Julie Calhoun, Cason and Nancy Callaway, Joe and Judith Colclasure, Dan and Sandra Cook, Betty Jane Daugherty, Claiborne and Elaine Deming, Tom and Mary Dillard, Robert and Mary Lynn Dudley, Jim Dyke and Helen Porter, Sally Foley, David Garner, Gaston Gibson, Wayne and Mary Ann Glenn, Wendell Hall and John HelmKamp, Fred and Helen Harrison, Jay and Patsy Hill, Harry and Jo Leggett, Henry and Marilyn Lile, Mike Mayton and Cathy Hamilton Mayton, Bruce McEntire, Chris and Lynn Parker, Duncan and Nancy Porter, Rick Smith and Susan Sims Smith, Richard and Peggy Smith, Reed and Becky Thompson, George and Sherry Worthen, Bill and Kathy Worthen.

Of the many individuals who have contributed in so many special ways, I would like to thank in particular: Lady Elizabeth Ashbrook, Viscount and Viscountess Ashbrook, David Baldwin, Chuck Bennet, Sandra Destaney and Daniel Blevens, Brent and Becky's Bulbs, Neal Brown, Dr. Tom Bruce, C. Douglas Buford, Gertrude Remmel Butler, Roy and Elizabeth Calder, Cantrell Gardens, Linda Chambers, Mr. and Mrs. Robert Doubleday, Sally Ferguson and The Netherlands Flower Bulb Information Center, Charles and Jane Foster, Glynwood Center, Kathlyn Graves, Mike Grey, Pam Hamblin, Hannah's Welding, Brian Hardin, Dr. and Mrs. Robert Hardin, Pat and Ann Herrington, Hocott's Garden Center, Pam Holden, Connie Hollenberg, Reverend Henry Hudson, Ken Hughs, Bertha Jackson, Tim Knox, Kevin, Bridget, Greta, and Julian Kresse, Judith LaBelle, Little Rock Rotary Club, Dr. Todd Longstaffe-Gowan, Larry Lowman, Joe Madonia, Jim Mauney, Sondra McCormack, Mitchell, Yoko, and Kess McSwain, Carl Miller, Brett Morgan, Mark and Cheri Nichols, Noah Ocken, Todd Quick, Bill Reishtein, Mr. and Mrs. Winthrop Rockefeller, John Scheeper's Bulb Company, Justin and Miles Slarks, Springhill Ornamental Concrete, Willie Swink, Gary Valen, Kathy Wagonitch, Dale Webb, Pat White, Katie Williams, Virginia Womack, and Susan, Rich, Sawyer, and Graceleigh Wright.

My appreciation also goes to Dwight Westerman, James Rucker, and Fred Chunn for their craftsmanship and help over the years to create my garden home.

I am particularly indebted to all of those who have assisted me in the garden as they helped to make the most of each season, none so important as my brother, Chris, who has always been there to lend a hand and a joyful heart.

I am grateful not only to my parents, but my grandparents, all members of a long line of farmers and gardeners, who taught me a love of the land and encouraged my artistic development.

Finally, I would like to thank all of those gardeners who have come before me, leaving me their designs and examples to study and follow, so I could discover the beautiful secrets of the garden.

SUGGESTED READING

PRACTICAL/TECHNICAL

Austin, David. *David Austin's English Roses—Glorious New Roses for American Gardens*. Boston: Little, Brown and Company, 1996.

Damrosh, Barbara. *The Garden Primer*. New York: Workman Publishing Company, 1988.

Hamilton, Geoff. *The Organic Garden Book*. New York: Crown Publishers, 1987.

Hobhouse, Penelope. *A Book of Gardening*. Boston: Little, Brown and Company, 1986.

Lacy, Allen, and Christopher Baker. *The Glory of Roses*. New York: Stewart, Tabori & Chang, 1990.

McHoy, Peter. *Pruning—A Practical Guide*. New York: Abbeville Press, 1993.

Pearson, Robert. *The Wisley Book of Gardening*. Collingridge Books, 1981.

Reich, Lee. *The Pruning Book*. Newton, Conn.: Taunton Press, 1997.

Sackville-West, Vita. *The Illustrated Garden Book*. New York: Atheneum, 1986.

Shapiro, Howard-Yana, and John Harrisson. *Gardening for the Future of Earth*. New York: Bantam Books, 2000.

Shoup, Michael G. *Roses in the Southern Garden*. Brenham, Tex.: Antique Rose Emporium, 2000.

Thomas, Graham. *The Art of Planting*. J.M. Dent and Sons, Limited, 1984.

Thorpe, Patricia. *Growing Pains: Time and Change in the Garden*. New York: Harcourt Brace, 1994.

Tripp, Kim E., and J. C. Raulston. *The Year in Trees—Superb Woody Plants for Four Season Gardens*. Portland, Ore.: Timber Press, 1995.

DESIGN

Brooks, John. *The Indoor Garden Book*. New York: Crown Publishers, 1986.

Chatto, Beth. *The Green Tapestry—Choosing and Grouping the Best Perennial Plants for Your Garden*. New York: Simon and Schuster, 1989.

Clark, Ethne, and George Wright. *English Topiary Gardens*. New York: Clarkson Potter, 1988.

De Bay, Philip, and James Bolton. *Garden Mania—The Ardent Gardener's Compendium of Design and Decoration*. London: Thames and Hudson, 2000.

Hadfield, Miles. *A History of British Gardening*. London: John Murray, 1979.

———. *Topiary and Ornamental Hedges*. A & C Black, Limited, 1971.

Harper, Pamela. *Designing with Perennials*. Sterling, 2001.

Harrison, Peter J. *Fences—Authentic Details for Design and Restoration*. New York: John Wiley and Sons, 1999.

Hobhouse, Penelope. *Colour in Your Garden*. Boston: Little, Brown and Company, 1985.

———. *Gardening Through the Ages*. New York: Simon and Schuster, 1992.

———. *Private Gardens of England*. New York: Harmony, 1986.

Jekyll, Gertrude. *Colour Schemes for the Flower Garden*. Woodbridge, England: Antique Collector's Club, 1982.

Jekyll, Gertrude, and Penelope Hobhouse. *Gertrude on Gardening*. David Godine Publisher, 1984.

Jekyll, Gertrude, and Lawrence Weaver. *Gardens for Small Country Houses*. Woodbridge, England: Antique Collector's Club, 1981.

Johnson, Hugh. *Principles of Gardening—The Practice of the Garden's Art*. New York: Simon and Schuster, 1996.

Lacy, Allen. *The Garden in Autumn*. New York: Atlantic Monthly Press, 1990.

McHoy, Peter. *Making the Most of a Small Garden*. Southwater Imprint of Amness Publishing Limited, 1994; distributed in U.S. by Ottenheimer Publishing, 2000.

Page, Russell. *The Education of a Gardener*. London: Collins, 1983.

Pope, Nori, and others. *Color by Design—Planting the Contemporary Garden*. San Francisco: Soma, 1998.

Seebohm, Caroline, and Christopher Simon Sykes. *Private Landscapes*. New York: Clarkson Potter, 1989.

Smith, Linda Joan. *Smith & Hawken Garden Structures*. New York: Workman Publishing Company, 2000.

Verey, Rosemary. *The Art of Planting*. Boston: Little, Brown and Company, 1990.

———. *The Garden in Winter*. New York: New York Graphic Society, 1988.

———. *The Scented Garden*. New York: Random House, 1987.

Weaver, Lawrence. *Houses and Gardens by E. L. Lutyens*. Woodbridge, England: Antique Collector's Club, 1981.

Wilder, Louise Beebe. *Color in My Garden*. New York: Atlantic Monthly Press, 1990.

———. *The Garden in Color*. New York: Macmillan, 1937.

GARDEN HISTORY

Antique Collector's Club. *Gardens in Edwardian England*. Newnes Books, 1985.

Betts, Edward M. *Thomas Jefferson's Garden Book*. American Philosophical Society, 1914.

Bryan, John M. *Biltmore Estate—The Most Distinguished Private Place*. New York: Rizzoli, 1994.

Clifford, Derek. *A History of Garden Design*. Praeger Publishers, 1963.

De'Medici, Lorenza. *The Renaissance of Italian Gardens*. New York: Fawcett Columbine, 1990.

Duchess of Devonshire. *The Garden at Chatsworth.* London: Francis Lincoln Limited, 1999.

Elliot, Brent. *Victorian Gardens.* B.T. Batsford Limited, 1986.

Gow, Ian. *Scottish Houses and Gardens—From the Archives of Country Life.* London: Aurum Press, 1997.

Griswold, Mac. *Washington's Gardens at Mount Vernon—Landscape of the Inner Man.* New York: Houghton Mifflin, 1999.

Griswold, Mac, and Eleanor Weller. *The Golden Age of American Gardens—Proud Owners, Private Estates, 1890–1940.* New York: Abrams, 1992.

Hatch, Peter J. *The Gardens of Thomas Jefferson's Monticello.* Charlottesville, Va.: Monticello, 1992. Reprint, 1998.

Hunt, John D., and Peter Willis. *The Genius of the Place.* New York: Harper and Row, 1975.

Jacques, David. *Georgian Gardens—The Reign of Nature.* Portland, Ore.: Timber Press, 1984.

Jefferson, Thomas, and Robert C. Baron. *The Garden and Farm Books of Thomas Jefferson.* Fulcrum Publishing, 1988.

Leighton, Ann. *Early American Gardens.* New York: Houghton Mifflin, 1970.

Longstaffe-Gowan, Todd. *The London Town Garden, 1700–1840.* London: Yale University Press, 2001.

Martin, Peter. *Pursuing Innocent Pleasures—The Gardening World of Alexander Pope.* Hamden, Conn.: Archon Books, 1984.

Masson, Georgina. *Italian Gardens.* Woodbridge, England: Antique Collector's Club, 1987.

Mosser, Monique, and Georges Teyssot. *The Architecture of Western Gardens.* Cambridge, Mass.: MIT Press, 1991.

Ottewill, David. *The Edwardian Garden.* New Haven: Yale University Press, 1989.

Plumptre, George. *Garden Ornament—Five Hundred Years of History and Practice.* London: Thames and Hudson, 1998.

Rybczynski, Witold. *A Clearing in the Distance—Frederick Law Olmsted and America in the Nineteenth Century.* New York: Scribner, 1999.

Schinz, Marina, and Gabrielle van Zuylen. *The Gardens of Russell Page.* New York: Stewart, Tabori and Chang, 1991.

Scott-James, Anne. *Sissinghurst—The Making of a Garden.* Michael Joseph Limited, 1974.

Shepherd, J. C., and G. A. Jellicoe. *Italian Gardens of the Renaissance.* Princeton: Princeton Architectural Press, 1986.

Strong, Roy. *The Renaissance Garden in England.* London: Thames and Hudson, 1979.

Stroud, Dorothy. *Capability Brown.* London: Country Life, 1957.

GENERAL

Dean, Jan. *The Gardener's Reading Guide.* New York: Facts on File, 1993.

Don, Monty, and Sarah Don. *Fork to Fork.* London: Conran Octopus Publishing Group, 1999.

Hunt, William L. *Southern Gardening.* Durham: Duke University Press, 1982.

Lacy, Allen. *The Gardener's Eye and Other Essays.* New York: Grove/Atlantic Inc., 1992.

Lawrence, Elizabeth. *Gardening for Love.* Durham: Duke University Press, 1987.

————. *The Little Bulbs—A Tale of Two Gardens.* Durham, N.C.: Duke University Press, 1986.

Lloyd, Christopher. *The Adventurous Gardener.* New York: Random House, 1983.

————. *Gardener Cook.* Minocqua, Wis.: Willow Creek Press, 1997.

————. *The Well-Tempered Garden.* New York: Random House, 1985.

Loewer, Peter. *The Evening Garden.* MacMillan Publishing Company, 1993.

Mitchell, Henry. *The Essential Earthman.* University of Indiana Press, 1981.

————. *Henry Mitchell on Gardening.* Boston: Houghton Mifflin Company, 1998.

National Gardens Scheme. *Gardens of England and Wales Open to the Public.* 1986.

Nichols, Beverly. *Down the Garden Path.* Woodbridge, England: Antique Collector's Club, 1997.

————. *How Does Your Garden Grow?* New York: Doubleday, Doran and Co., 1935.

————. *A Village in a Valley.* London: Jonathan Cape, Limited, 1934.

Nicolson, Philippa. *V. Sackville-West's Garden Book.* London: Michael Joseph, 1968.

Pereire, Anita, and Gabrielle Van Zuylen. *Gardens of France.* New York: Harmony Books, 1983.

Perenyi, Eleanor. *Green Thoughts—A Writer in the Garden.* New York: Random House, 1981.

Pettingill, Amos. *The White Flower Farm Garden Book.* New York: Knopf, 1971.

Pollan, Michael. *Second Nature: A Gardener's Education.* New York: Atlantic Monthly Press, 1991.

Schinz, Marina. *Visions of Paradise.* New York: Stewart Tabori, 1985.

White, Katherine. *Onward and Upward in the Garden.* New York: Farrar, Straus, Giroux, 1979.

Whiteside, Katherine. *Antique Flowers.* New York: Villard Books, 1988.

Zuazua Jenkins, Mary. *National Geographic's Guide to America's Public Gardens.* National Geographic Society, 1998.

REFERENCE

Armitage, Allan M. *Armitage's Garden Perennials—A Color Encyclopedia.* Portland, Ore.: Timber Press, 2000.

Armitage, Allen. *Herbaceous Perennial Plants.* Varsity Press, 1989.

Beales, Peter. *Classic Roses—An Illustrated Encyclopaedia and Grower's Manual of Old Roses, Shrub Roses and Climbers.* New York: Henry Holt & Company, 1997.

Dirr, Michael. *Manual of Woody Landscape Plants.* Champaign, Ill.: Stipes, 1978.

Morris, Alistair. *Antiques from the Garden.* Woodbridge, England: Garden Art Press, 1998.

Phillips, Roger, and Martyn E. Rix. *The Bulb Book—A Photographic Guide to Over 800 Hardy Bulbs.* Pan Books, 1977.

————. *The Random House Book of Roses.* New York: Random House, 1988.

Staff of the L. H. Bailey Hortorium, Cornell University. *Hortus Third.* New York: Macmillan, 1976.

Taylor, Norman. *Taylor's Guides.* Boston: Houghton Mifflin. Annual.

Wyman, Donald. *Wyman's Gardening Encyclopedia.* New York: Macmillan, 1971.

GLOSSARY

ACIDIC SOIL Garden soil having a pH below 7.

ALCOVE A secluded garden structure.

ALKALINE SOIL Garden soil having a pH above 7.

ALLÉE Literally, from the French word a "way," but in gardening used to denote a passage, or approach, lined with trees, sometimes clipped to form a smooth wall.

ANNUAL A plant that completes its life cycle within a year or less, such as zinnias and petunias.

ARBOR An open-ended structure with latticework sides and vines trained over the top to create a leafy canopy. In garden design most often used as an entry, as covered seating, or as a method to frame a view.

ARMILLARY SPHERE A globe-like device used in ancient times to represent the celestial sphere. A popular garden ornament.

ASYMMETRY The opposite of symmetry; using a different shape of like mass to create balance on each side of an axis.

AXIS A sight line in the garden that points to an object or view in the distance. Also refers to the main stem or branch from which leaves and flowers grow.

BALUSTRADE A series of short vertical posts supporting a rail, used as decorative support along the edge of balconies, staircases, and the roofline of buildings.

BASIN A naturally occurring or artificially created area where water flows from a stream into an enclosed area to create a pool or pond. A wide and shallow dish made of stone.

BELVEDERE A building or part of a building designed to overlook an attractive vista.

BIENNIAL A plant that completes its life cycle over two years. The first year it produces only foliage and the second year it flowers, fruits, and dies. An example is foxglove.

BOG A marsh garden.

BORROWED VIEW To incorporate into a garden design elements of a distant view, especially those occurring naturally in the landscape.

BOWER A leafy shelter created with intertwined boughs of trees or vines trained over an arbor.

CAPSTONE A stone topping a pillar or a wall to give it a finished look.

CARPET BED A flower bed designed to resemble a carpet by using low-growing plants of even height that are arranged in the intricate patterns of a carpet.

CASCADE A fall of water designed to flow over a succession of steps or rocks.

CISTERN A man-made reservoir used to collect and store rainwater for irrigation purposes.

CLOCHE A cover used to protect young plants from frost or cold, usually bell shaped.

COLONNADE A row of columns set at a regular interval, most often used to support a roof structure.

COLUMNAR A plant whose branches grow upright, creating a column-like effect.

COPING Finishing layer of stone on a wall or around a pool, usually positioned on a slant to shed water.

COPPICE A medieval method of creating more vigorous growth by cutting back a tree or shrub almost to the ground.

CRENELLATE To shape a hedge with repeated square indentations like a battlement.

CRINKLE-CRANKLE A serpentine-shaped wall or hedge.

CULTIVAR Cultivated variety. A plant created through selective hybridization that maintains its unique properties under cultivation.

DELL A secluded valley or hollow.

EN MASSE To plant in large groupings.

ESPALIER A series of trees whose branches are trained to grow flat against a wall, on a trellis, or on a structure of lines and stakes, to create a hedge.

FASTIGIATE Trees and shrubs with branches that are upright and close together creating a columnar shape. An example is the Lombardy poplar.

FINIAL A sculptured ornament used as a cap for a post, pillar, or similar structure.

FLAGSTONE A flat stone used for paths, terraces, etc.

FOLLY A garden structure, often extravagant, implemented for visual effect—"to fool the eye."

GARTH An enclosed garden.

GAZEBO A freestanding open structure with a roof.

GLADE An open grassy field surrounded by woods.

GLAUCOUS Bluish-gray or bluish-white in color. Sometimes used to refer to blooms whitened by a fine powdery substance.

GRAFTING A method of propagation where the shoot of one

plant is inserted into another with the intention of the two growing together into a single plant. This method is used on trees, shrubs, and roses.

GROTTO A structure built to resemble a natural cave. Used to create mystery in a garden.

GROVE A small group of trees.

HA-HA A hidden ditch with one sloping wall and one vertical wall used in place of a fence to contain animals. Use of a ha-ha rather than a fence allows for an unbroken view of the landscape. An example can be seen in use at many modern zoos.

HERBACEOUS A plant with little or no woody tissue. A plant that dies back to its roots in winter. Perennials are often referred to as herbaceous.

HERM A garden ornament consisting of a carved bust on a tall pedestal.

HORTUS CONCLUSUS Latin for "enclosed garden." A medieval garden enclosed by walls, usually rectangular in shape.

HYBRID A cross between two different species resulting in a plant that contains characteristics of both parents.

JARDINIERE A stoneware planter.

KNOT A garden consisting of dwarf shrubs, herbs, and flowers designed in an intricate geometric pattern, or knot.

LOGGIA A covered arcade that is open on one or more sides and often attached to a building.

MOUNT A small man-made hill in a garden created to provide a view of the countryside.

NATURALIZE To allow a plant to grow undisturbed and reproduce as it would in the wild thus giving the area a natural look. Daffodils naturalize well.

NEUTRAL Garden soil that is neither acidic nor alkaline.

NICHE A recessed area in a wall for holding garden ornaments.

OBELISK A tall, thin structure or pillar that tapers to a point or ends in a pyramid. Used as a focal point in the garden.

OCULUS A round window or circular opening in a garden wall or at the top of a dome.

ORCHARD An area in the garden devoted to growing fruit or nut trees.

ORNAMENT A nonstructural element of decoration in the garden, such as an urn, statuary, or a birdbath.

ORNAMENTAL Showy landscape plants grown in a garden to add visual interest rather than to serve a practical purpose.

PALING A fence made out of pointed sticks, pickets, or stakes.

PARTERRE A garden where the beds and paths are laid out to form a pattern.

PEDESTAL A base or foot for a column, statue, or ornament.

PERENNIAL A plant that lives for more than two years, literally to come back year after year.

PERGOLA An open structure made up of columns supporting a trellis roof on which plants are trained to grow.

PERISTYLE A structure or court surrounded by columns.

PH Measure of acidity or alkalinity of garden soil.

PLEACHING Interweaving the branches of a row of well-spaced woody plants to create a dense hedge. Often used with trees such as lime or hornbeam.

PLINTH A square or column-shaped base for ornaments.

POLLARD A tree that has been repeatedly cut back to the main trunk each year. This process creates a thick trunk with a knotted top.

PORTICO A covered porch or walkway with a roof supported by columns.

POTAGER A formal kitchen garden.

PROSTRATE To grow low to the ground. Prostrate plants have a flat, spreading habit.

PUTTO An image of a small child depicted as a winged angel, a popular subject for garden sculpture, fountains, and reliefs.

RILL A stream.

RONDEL A rounded or circular bed space.

RUIN A dilapidated structure with historical connotations. A popular feature in larger gardens to create mystery and a sense of time.

RUSTICATED Structures and stonework that have been naturally or artificially roughened to give a more bucolic look.

SCAPE A scene or a view. Also refers to a leafless flower stalk.

SPECIES A group of plants with the same unique traits. To regenerate true from seed.

SPORT When a plant produces a branch that differs in appearance from the rest of the plant due to a natural genetic change. A plant produced through the propagation of such a branch. Many roses are sports of older varieties.

STANDARD A woody plant trained to have a treelike form with a single vertical stem and rounded top.

SYMMETRY Correspondence in size, shape, and position of parts on opposite sides of an axis.

TROMPE L'OEIL A painting that sets up the illusion of seeing reality.

TONSURE To shape evergreen shrubs by clipping.

TOPIARY A garden or plant trimmed or trained into three-dimensional shapes.

TROUGH A container for holding water, long and narrow in shape and generally shallow.

TUFA A porous type of stone created as a deposit from a spring or stream. A porous rock able to sustain plant life.

UMBEL A cluster of blooms that radiate from a single stalk, umbrella in shape. Geraniums have umbel bloom clusters.

URN A vase with a foot or pedestal.

VISTA A long view as seen through intervening objects such as trees. A view through a narrow passageway opening to a larger scene.

WATTLE A fence or wall made of intertwined branches.

GARDENS TO VISIT

UNITED STATES

BELLINGRATH GARDENS
12401 Bellingrath Gardens Road
Theodore, AL 36582
Tel.: 334-973-2217
Open all year, daily.

FILOLI
Canada Road
Woodside, CA 94062
Tel.: 650-364-8300
Fax: 650-366-7836
www.filoli.org
Open mid-February through the end
of October, Tuesday through
Saturday.

GANNA WALSKA LOTUSLAND
695 Ashley Road
Santa Barbara, CA 93108
Tel.: 805-969-9990
Open mid-February through mid-
November, Wednesday through
Saturday. Reservations required.

**HUNTINGTON BOTANICAL
GARDENS**
1151 Oxford Road
San Marino, CA 91108
Tel.: 818-405-2141
www.huntington.org
Open all year, Tuesday through
Sunday. Closed holidays.

**SANTA BARBARA BOTANIC
GARDEN**
1212 Mission Canyon Road
Santa Barbara, CA 93105
Tel.: 805-682-4726
www.santabarbarabotanicgarden.org
Open all year, daily. Closed
holidays.

**GERTRUDE JEKYLL GARDEN AT
THE GLEBE HOUSE MUSEUM**
Hollow Road
Woodbury, CT 06798
Tel.: 203-263-2855
Open April through December,
Wednesday through Sunday.

NEMOURS GARDENS
Rockland Road
Wilmington, DE 19803
Tel.: 302-651-6912
Open May through November,
Tuesday through Sunday.

VIZCAYA
3251 South Miami Avenue
Miami, FL 33131
Tel.: 305-250-9133
Open all year, daily. Closed
Christmas.

CALLAWAY GARDENS
US Highway 27
Pine Mountain, GA 31822
Tel.: 800-225-5292 or 706-663-2281
Fax: 706-663-5068
www.callawaygardens.com
Open all year, daily.

CANTIGNY
1 South, 151 Winfield Road
Wheaton, IL 60187
Tel.: 630-668-5161
Open Tuesday through Sunday,
March through December; Friday
through Sunday, February.

CHICAGO BOTANIC GARDEN
1000 Lake Cook Road
Glencoe, IL 60022
Tel.: 847-835-5440
www.chicago-botanic.org
Open all year. Closed Christmas.

AFTON VILLA
St. Francisville, LA 70775
Tel.: 225-635-6773
Open March through June, October
through November, daily.

LONGUE VUE GARDENS
7 Bamboo Road
New Orleans, LA 70124
Tel.: 504-488-5488
Fax: 504-486-7015
Email: info@longuevue.com
www.longuevue.com
Open all year. Closed holidays.

ROSEDOWN PLANTATION
12501 State Highway 10
St. Francisville, LA 70775
Tel.: 225-635-3332
Open all year, daily.

LADEW TOPIARY GARDENS
3535 Jarrettsville Pike
Monkton, MD 21111
Tel.: 410-557-9570
Fax: 410-557-7763
www.ladewgardens.com
Open mid-April through October.

WILLIAM PACA GARDEN
186 Prince George Street
Annapolis, MD 21401
Tel.: 410-263-5553
Open Monday through Sunday,
March through December; Friday,
Saturday, and Monday, January and
February. Closed Thanksgiving and
Christmas.

**THE ARNOLD ARBORETUM OF
HARVARD UNIVERSITY**
125 Arborway
Jamaica Plain, MA 02130
Tel.: 617-524-1718
www.arboretum.harvard.edu
Open all year, daily.

**ISABELLA STEWART GARDNER
MUSEUM**
280 The Fenway
Boston, MA 02115
Tel.: 617-566-1401
www.gardnermuseum.org
Open all year, Tuesday through
Sunday. Closed holidays.

NAUMKEAG
Prospect Hill
Stockbridge, MA 01262
Tel.: 413-298-3239
Open early May to October, daily.

**CRANBROOK HOUSE AND
GARDENS**
380 Lone Pine Road, Box 801
Bloomfield Hills, MI 48303
Tel.: 248-645-3149
Open May through October, daily.

MISSOURI BOTANICAL GARDEN
4344 Shaw Boulevard
St. Louis, MO 63110
Tel.: 314-577-5100
www.mobot.org
Open all year, daily.

**SKYLANDS BOTANICAL
GARDEN**
Ringwood State Park
Ringwood, NJ 07456
Tel.: 973-962-7527
Open all year, daily.

**BANDELIER GARDEN (THE
GARDEN AT EL ZAGUAN)**
545 Canyon Road
Santa Fe, NM 87501
Tel.: 505-983-2567
Open all year, Monday through
Saturday.

BROOKLYN BOTANIC GARDEN
1000 Washington Avenue
Brooklyn, NY 11225
Tel.: 718-622-4433
www.bbg.org
Open all year, Tuesday through
Sunday.

THE CLOISTERS
Fort Tyron Park
New York, NY 10040
Tel.: 212-923-3700
www.fieldtrip.com/ny/29233700
Open all year, Tuesday through
Sunday. Closed holidays.

NEW YORK BOTANICAL
GARDEN
200th Street and Kazimiroff
Boulevard
Bronx, NY 10458
Tel.: 718-817-8700
www.nybg.org
Open all year, Tuesday through
Sunday and on Monday holidays.
Closed Thanksgiving and
Christmas.

OLD WESTBURY GARDENS
71 Old Westbury Road
Old Westbury, NY 11568
Tel.: 516-333-0048
Open May through December,
Wednesday through Monday.
Closed Christmas.

STONECROP GARDENS
RR2, Box 371
Cold Spring, NY 10516
Tel.: 914-265-2000
Open mid-April through October,
Tuesday, Wednesday, and Friday.
By appointment only.

WAVE HILL
West 249th Street and
Independence Avenue
Bronx, NY 10471
Tel.: 718-549-3200
www.wavehill.org
Open all year, Tuesday through
Sunday. Closed holidays.

J. C. RAULSTON ARBORETUM
North Carolina State University
4301 Beryl Road
Raleigh, NC 27606
Tel.: 919-515-3132

www.ncsu.edu/jcraulstonarboretum
Open all year, daily.

SARAH P. DUKE GARDENS
Duke University and Academy
Roads
Durham, NC 27402
Tel.: 919-684-3698
Open all year, daily.

TYRON PALACE GARDENS
610 Pollock Street
New Bern, NC 28563
Tel.: 919-514-4900
Open all year, daily. Closed
holidays.

LONGWOOD GARDENS
US 1
Kennett Square, PA 19438
Tel.: 610-388-1000
www.longwoodgardens.org
Open all year, daily.

MIDDLETON PLACE
Ashley River Road
Pinesville, SC 29414
Tel.: 803-556-6020
Open all year, daily.

THE HERMITAGE
Home of Andrew Jackson
4580 Rachel's Lane
Hermitage, TN 37076
Tel.: 615-889-2941
Open all year, daily.
Closed Thanksgiving, Christmas,
and the third week of January.

BAYOU BEND COLLECTION
AND GARDENS
Museum of Fine Arts
1 Westcott Street
Houston, TX 77007
Tel.: 713-639-7750
Open Tuesday through Sunday,
January to February, April to July,
September to November. Call for
hours in December, March, and
August.

DALLAS ARBORETUM AND
BOTANICAL GARDEN
8525 Garland Road
Dallas, TX 75218
Tel.: 214-327-8263
www.dallasarboretum.org
Open all year, daily.

FORT WORTH BOTANIC
GARDEN
3220 Botanic Garden Boulevard
Fort Worth, TX 76107
Tel.: 817-871-7689 or 817-871-7686
www.fortworthgov.org/pacs/
botgarden
Open all year, daily.

COLONIAL WILLIAMSBURG
Colonial Parkway
Williamsburg, VA 23187
Tel.: 757-229-1000 or
1-800-HISTORY
Open all year, daily.

GUNSTON HALL PLANTATION
Mason Neck, VA 22079
Tel.: 703-550-9220
Fax: 703-550-9480
Email: Historic@GunstonHall.org
www.gunstonhall.org
Open all year except holidays.

MONTICELLO
P.O. Box 316
Charlottesville, VA 22902
Tel.: 434-984-9800 or
434-984-9822
www.monticello.org/grounds
Open all year. Closed Christmas.

MOUNT VERNON ESTATE AND
GARDENS
George Washington Memorial
Parkway
Mount Vernon, VA 22121
Tel.: 703-780-2000
www.mountvernon.org
Open all year, daily.

OATLANDS PLANTATION
Oatlands Plantation Lane
Leesburg, VA 20175
Tel.: 703-777-3174
Open April to mid-December,
Monday through Sunday. Closed
Thanksgiving.

BISHOP'S GARDEN
Washington National Cathedral
Massachusetts and Wisconsin
Avenue, NW
Washington, DC 20016
Tel.: 202-537-2937
Open all year, daily.

DUMBARTON OAKS
1703 32nd Street, NW
Washington, DC 20007
Tel.: 202-339-6401
www.doaks.org
Open all year, daily, except holidays.

U. S. NATIONAL ARBORETUM
3501 New York Avenue, NE
Washington, DC 20002
Tel.: 202-245-2726
www.usna.usda.gov
Open all year. Closed Christmas.

GREAT BRITAIN

ARLEY HALL AND GARDENS
Great Budworth, Cheshire
England CW9 6NA
Tel.: 01565 777353
Fax: 01 565 777465
www.arleyestate.zuunet.co.uk
Open Tuesday through Sunday,
mid-April to end of September;
weekends in October.

BODNANT GARDEN
Tal-y-Cafn, Colwyn Bay
Gwynedd, Wales LL28 5RE
Tel.: 01 492 650460
Open mid-March to October, daily.

CHATSWORTH
Bakewell, Derbyshire
England DE45 1PP
Tel.: 01 246 565300
Fax: 01 246 583536
www.chatsworth.org
Open March to October, daily.

CHOLMONDELEY CASTLE
GARDENS
Malpas, Cheshire
England SY14 8AH
Tel.: 01829 720383
Open April to September,
Wednesday, Thursday, Sunday, and
bank holiday Mondays.

HARDWICK HALL
Doe Lea, Chesterfield
Derbyshire, England S44 5QJ
Tel.: 01 246 850430
Open end of March to end of
October, Wednesday, Thursday,
Saturday, Sunday, and bank holiday
Mondays. Country park open all
year, dawn to dusk.

HESTERCOMBE HOUSE GARDENS
Cheddon Fitzpaine, Taunton
Somerset, England TA2 8LG
Tel.: 01 823 413923
Fax: 01823 413747
www.hestercombegardens.com
Open all year, daily.

HEVER CASTLE AND GARDENS
Hever, Edenbridge, Kent
England TN8 7NG
Tel.: 01 732 865224
www.hevercastle.co.uk
Open March to November, daily.

HIDCOTE MANOR
Gloucestershire
England GL55 6LR
Tel.: 01 386 438333
Fax: 01 386 438817
www.nationaltrust.org.uk/hidcote
Open late March to end of October,
Monday, Wednesday, Thursday,
Saturday, and Sunday. Also open
Tuesdays in June and July.

KIFTSGATE COURT GARDENS
Chipping Campden,
Gloucestershire
England GL55 6LW
Tel./fax: 01 386 438777
www.kiftsgate.co.uk
Open April, May, August, and
September, Wednesdays,
Thursdays, Sundays, and bank
holiday Mondays.

KNIGHTSHAYES COURT
Bolham, Tiverton, Devon
England EX16 7RQ
Tel.: 01 884 254665
Open March to October, daily.

MOTTISFONT ABBEY GARDEN
Mottisfont, Hampshire
England SO51 0LP
Tel.: 01 794 340757
Open late March to early
November, Saturday through
Wednesday.

NEWBY HALL AND GARDENS
North Yorkshire
England HG4 5AE
Tel.: 01 423 322583
Fax: 01 423 324452
www.newbyhall.com

Open April to September, Tuesday
through Sunday and bank holiday
Mondays.

NYMANS GARDEN
Nymans, Handcross,
nr Haywards Heath, West Sussex
England RH17 6EB
Tel.: 01 444 400321
Open March to October,
Wednesday through Sunday and
bank holiday Mondays; open
Saturday and Sunday only from
November to February.

PENSHURST PLACE
Penshurst, Tonbridge, Kent
England TN11 8DG
Tel.: 01 892 870307
Fax: 01 892 870866
www.penshurstplace.com
Open daily from April to November;
open weekends in March.

SUDELEY CASTLE
Winchcombe, Gloucestershire
England GL54 5JD
Tel.: 01 242 602308
Fax: 01 242 602959
www.sudeleycastle.co.uk
Open April to end of October, daily.

**WAKEHURST PLACE
ROYAL HORTICULTURAL
SOCIETY GARDEN**
Ardingly, Haywards Heath
West Sussex, England RH17 6TN
Tel.: 01 444 894066
www.rbgkew.org.uk
Open all year, daily (except
December 25 and January 1).

**WISLEY ROYAL
HORTICULTURAL SOCIETY
GARDEN**
Wisley, Surrey
England GU23 6QB
Tel.: 01 483 224234
www.rhs.org.uk
Open all year except Christmas Day.
Sundays from March to October
reserved for RHS members and
guests.

ITALY

BOBOLI GARDENS
Pitti Palace, Florence
Tel.: 055 218741
Open all year, daily (except first and
last Monday of each month).

VILLA GAMBERAIA
Via del Rossellino, 72
50135 Settignano, Florence
Tel.: 055 697205 or 055 697090
Fax: 055 697090
Email: villagam@tin.it
www.webspace.it/villagamberaia
Open daily.

VILLA I TATTI
The Harvard University Center for
Italian Renaissance Studies
Via di Vincigliata, 26
50135 Florence
Tel.: 055 603 251
Fax: 055 603 383
www.vit.ittati.it
Garden visits need to be booked in
advance.

VILLA LA PIETRA
Via Bolognese, 120
50139 Florence
Fax: 055 472 725
Open by appointment. The garden
is owned by New York University.

VILLA LANTE
Bagnaia, Lazio
Tel.: 0761 288 008
Open all year, daily; closed holidays.

**VILLA MEDICI CASTELLO
(VILLA REALE)**
Castello, Tuscany
Tel.: 0583 30108 or 0583 30009
Open all year, daily; closed on
second and third Monday of each
month.

VILLA TORRIGIANI
Camigliano, Lucca
Tel.: 0583 928008
Fax: 0583 928041
Open March through October.

FRANCE

LE BOIS DES MOUTIERS
Route de l'église
76119 Varengeville-sur-Mer
Tel.: 02 85 10 02
Fax: 02 85 46 98
Open mid-March through mid-
November, daily.

CHAUMONT-SUR-LOIRE
Château de Chaumont
41150 Chaumont-sur-Loire
Tel.: 02 54 51 26 26
Fax: 02 54 20 91 16
Email: chaumontsurloire@
chateauxcountry.com
www.chateauxandcountry.com/
chateaux/chaumontsurloire
Open mid-June through late
October (Festival of Gardens).

EYRIGNAC
Les Jardins du Manoir D'Eyrignac
24590 Salignac, Aquitaine
Tel.: 05 53 28 99 71
Fax: 05 53 30 39 89
www.uehha.org/fr/Aquitaine/
eyrignac_en.htm
Open all year, daily.

**JARDIN BOTANIQUE DU
CHÂTEAU DE VAUVILLE**
50440 Vauville, Normandy
Tel.: 02 33 52 71 41
Fax: 02 33 52 72 31
Email: jbotvauville@wanadoo.fr
www.uehha.org/fr/Basse-
_Normandie/vauville_en.htm
Open May through September,
Sunday through Tuesday; open
Saturdays in June.

LE LABYRINTHE
Jardin des Cinq Sens
Chateau d'Yvoire
Rue du Lac, 74140 Yvoire
Tel.: 04 50 72 88 80
Fax: 04 50 72 90 80
Email: mail@jardin5sens.net
www.jardin5sens.net
Open April to October, daily.

PARC ANDRÉ CITROEN
Paris
Open all year, daily.

INDEX

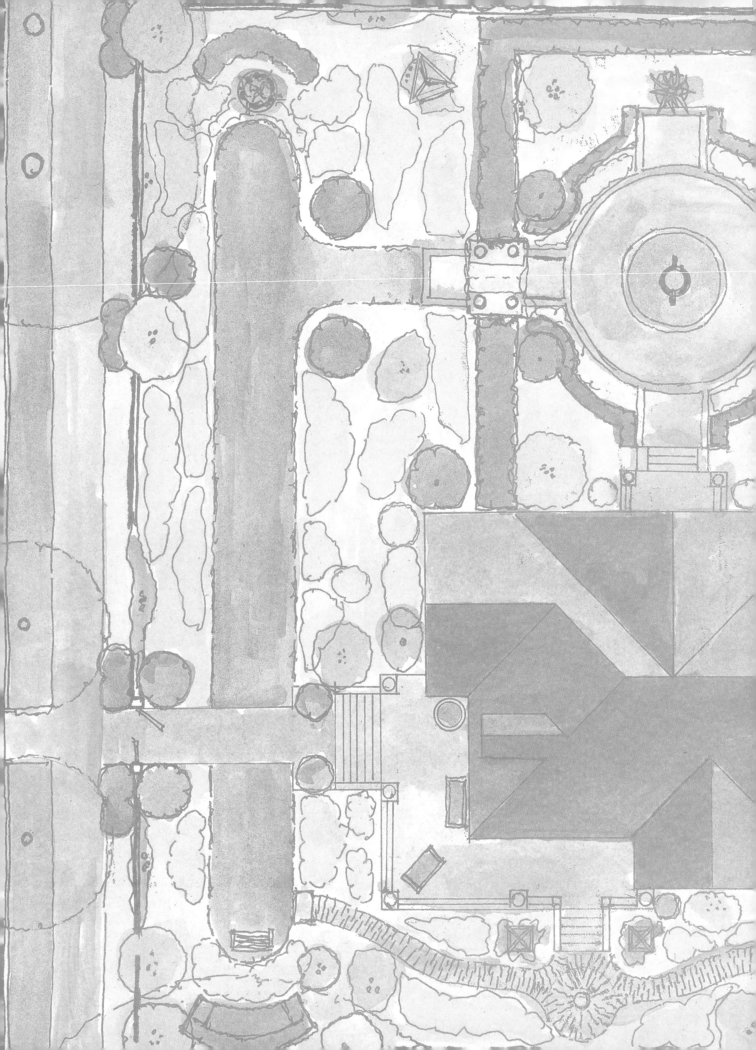